iOS eCommerce App Development with Parse

Liangjun Jiang

Apress®

iOS eCommerce App Development with Parse

ISBN-13 (pbk): 978-1-4842-1318-6

ISBN-13 (electronic): 978-1-4842-1317-9

Managing Director: Welmoed Spahr
Lead Editor: Louise Corrigan
Technical Reviewer: Bruce Wade
Editorial Board: Steve Anglin, Louise Corrigan, Jonathan Gennick, Robert Hutchinson,
    Michelle Lowman, James Markham, Susan McDermott, Matthew Moodie, Jeffrey Pepper,
    Douglas Pundick, Ben Renow-Clarke, Gwenan Spearing, Steve Weiss
Coordinating Editor: Mark Powers
Copy Editor: Karen Jameson
Compositor: SPi Global
Indexer: SPi Global
Artist: SPi Global

Distributed to the book trade worldwide by Springer Science+Business Media New York, 233 Spring Street, 6th Floor, New York, NY 10013. Phone 1-800-SPRINGER, fax (201) 348-4505, e-mail orders-ny@springer-sbm.com, or visit www.springeronline.com. Apress Media, LLC is a California LLC and the sole member (owner) is Springer Science + Business Media Finance Inc (SSBM Finance Inc). SSBM Finance Inc is a Delaware corporation.

For information on translations, please e-mail rights@apress.com, or visit www.apress.com.

Apress and friends of ED books may be purchased in bulk for academic, corporate, or promotional use. eBook versions and licenses are also available for most titles. For more information, reference our Special Bulk Sales–eBook Licensing web page at www.apress.com/bulk-sales.

Any source code or other supplementary materials referenced by the author in this text is available to readers at www.apress.com/9781484213186. For detailed information about how to locate your book's source code, go to www.apress.com/source-code/. Readers can also access source code at SpringerLink in the Supplementary Material section for each chapter.

Contents at a Glance

Contents

About the Author

Liangjun Jiang is a mobile app software engineer from Austin, Texas. Jiang has a PhD in electrical engineering from the University of Central Florida and an MS and BE from Zhejiang University, China. His software experience has led him to utilize many different technologies, including Objective-C, Java, JavaScript and, of course, iOS and Android. Aside from hacking codes, he enjoys spending time with his family, as well as running, golfing, and playing tennis.

About the Technical Reviewer

Bruce Wade is the founder of Warply Designed Inc.
(www.warplydesigned.com), a company specializing in using
game technology for real-world applications. He has more
than 16 years of software development experience with a
strong focus on 2D/3D animation and interactive applications,
primarily using Apple technology.

Introduction

In this comprehensive guide to creating an e-commerce iOS app using Objective-C and Parse, the most popular and powerful Backend as a Service (BaaS) provider. I will walk you through every step—from collecting requirements; prototyping the visual interface; setting up the project with Xcode and Parse; creating the data model with Parse; presenting, searching, filtering, and favoriting products; managing the shopping bag; processing the payment; and managing a user account—always with security best practices in mind.

The book uses a complete and functioning e-commerce iPhone app as the example, along with various Parse products, to present the most popular use case of an e-commerce mobile app, such as user account creation, logging in with Facebook, user e-mail verification, paying with Stripe and Apple Pay, sending e-mail with Mailgun, and managing customer payment methods and order history.

Chapter 1 presents a broad requirements overview of an e-commerce iOS app, based on the Apple Store iPhone app.

Chapter 2 walks you through the process of using Xcode to prototype the e-commerce iPhone app with minimum code.

Chapter 3 gives you an overview of what Parse offers, and Chapter 4 explains how to set up this project, including services, such as Facebook Developer, Mailgun, and Stripe, which you will need later.

Chapters 5, 6, and 7 detail how to build product categories, product lists, and product details, along with features such as searching, filtering, etc.

Chapters 8 and 9 present the user interface and functionality of signing up and logging in a user and Facebook Login.

Chapters 10–14 detail how to build a shopping bag, how to charge a credit card, or how to let a user pay with Apple Pay. It includes some back-end code that we have to write.

Chapter 15 focuses on a user's account. This is the place that the user can log out, view an order history, and create a favorites product list.

Chapter 16 demonstrates how to add products. This is a hidden feature available only to an admin.

Chapter 17 is a bonus chapter. I show you how to use push notification as a way of promotion.

Chapter 18 gives details about security.

Chapter 19 lists some extra features from Parse that you can use to make your product better, including e-mail verification, password reset, Parse Analytics, and Crash Reports.

Audience

This book is for experienced iOS developers confident with Objective-C, iOS, Xcode, and some back-end knowledge; and for those interested in building an e-commerce iPhone app. In other words, intermediate knowledge of iOS development and object-oriented programming is assumed, and basic knowledge of e-commerce principles will also be of benefit.

If you don't have the experience of implementing a fully functional back end but still want to build a web services–based iPhone app, this book is for you. This book is also great for experienced mobile app developers wanting to enhance their skills and learn new tools.

What You Will Learn

From this book, you will learn the following:

1. What it takes to develop a functional e-commerce iPhone app

2. Parse and its products and how it can help you accelerate your app development

3. How to incorporate a Stripe payment gateway and Mailgun e-mail service

4. How to develop a scalable app that is also easy to maintain

5. What you need to secure your app and user data

6. How to extend the examples from this book to match the needs of your own app

iOS SDK Version and Source Code for the example

This book has been written to work with the latest versions of Xcode, iOS, Parse, and Stripe SDKs. Be sure to download the latest and greatest source code archive for examples from this book's page at http://apress.com/9781484213186. We'll update the code as new versions of the SDK are released, so be sure to check the site periodically.

Requirements

This book is about understanding the steps involved in designing, architecting, building, and publishing an e-commerce mobile application. When using the term *e-commerce* in this book, I am referring to selling products and collecting money from customers. I will not cover how to put ads in a mobile app or provide a referral link when a customer makes a purchase on other sites or mobile apps.

This book is about about building a mobile app that enables users to purchase products. It involves collecting customers' names, addresses, and credit card information. The money collected will be transferred into a bank account, and the products ordered will subsequently be shipped and delivered. As challenging as this sounds, it's easier than having registered legal business entities take care of these details.

This book assumes that you have some iOS programming knowledge. However, if you are a business owner planning to sell your products through a mobile app and are thinking about hiring an iOS developer or a consulting firm to accomplish your goal, this book will help you to understand the process, the required steps, and the effort involved.

In this chapter you will learn about:

- Common requirements for an e-commerce mobile app
- Prerequisites for building, testing, and publishing iOS apps

Common Application Requirements

What's your favorite e-commerce iOS app? Before you think too hard, consider this: every iPhone, iPad, and iPod Touch has one built in; it's the Apple Store app (see Figure 1-1). If you have never used it before, now is the time to explore it.

Figure 1-1. The iPhone Apple Store app icon

The Apple Store App

At the time of writing, the Apple Store iOS app had received 53,706 reviews with an average rating of 3.5 stars. Version 3.5, released on September 24, 2015, has an average of 4 stars.

The app has five top-level content categories (see Figure 1-2):

- Featured
- Shop
- Stores
- Account
- Cart

Figure 1-2. The five content categories of the Apple Store iPhone app

Featured

The Featured category is the place for highlighting products (such as Apple Watch, for example). Tapping a highlighted product reveals the product detail.

Shop

The Shop category displays all product categories in the Apple Store at a glance, including Mac computers, iPhone, Apple Watch, and Accessories. The Shop screen also includes a search bar at the top of the screen (see Figure 1-3).

Figure 1-3. Shop category of the Apple Store iPhone app

Tap a product category, and you will see all products that belong to this category. Note also that the title of the product list screen matches the category name. For example, if you tap the "Mac" category on the Shop screen, "Mac" appears as the title of the Mac computers list screen.

Tapping an item on the product list screen displays the product detail screen. In addition to the well-chosen product images, you will also see a product description, the price, an "ADD TO CART" button, and an action button at the top of the current screen (see Figure 1-4). You might also see an option to customize a product, which will lead you to more screens.

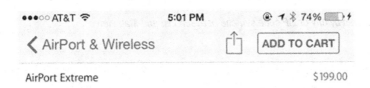

Figure 1-4. The "ADD TO CART" button at the top of a product detail screen

Other features include an availability check and the ability to read more about a product's features, rate and review a product, and ask questions and find answers (Q&A) (see Figure 1-5).

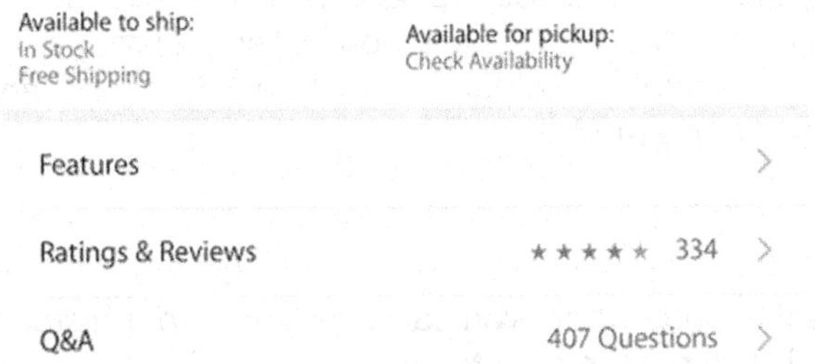

Available to ship: In Stock Free Shipping	Available for pickup: Check Availability	
Features		>
Ratings & Reviews	★ ★ ★ ★ ★ 334	>
Q&A	407 Questions	>

Figure 1-5. More features on a product detail screen

Stores

The Stores category directs you to the nearest Apple stores. The app also detects whether Location Services are turned on and, if not, notifies you (see Figure 1-6).

Figure 1-6. Location Services requirement while using the Apple Store app

The app also provides a search feature that enables you to find stores by city or ZIP code and browse stores in list form or see them on a map (see Figure 1-7).

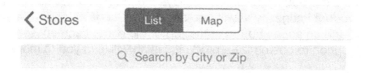

Figure 1-7. Find a stores by city or ZIP code switche between List and Map views

Account

The Account category is where you manage your customer profile, such as favorites, order history, reservation with a genius at the Apple Store, and settings. This category is only accessible if you have an account and are logged in to the Apple Store. If you don't have an account or have not logged in, the app only displays the general about information such as terms, privacy policy, and app version as well as a button that asks you to log in.

Favorites

The Favorites category lists the items you previously "favored" (by tapping the heart button on a product detail page). Tap "Favorites," and you will see a product list. You can also edit the list, such as deleting a product. Another nice feature is that you can change views to view your favorites in list or grid mode.

Orders

The Orders category is the place where you can view your order history (see Figure 1-8). By default, the list is sorted from most recent to oldest.

Ordered On
April 10, 2015

Order #
W458386038

Apple Watch Sport 42mm Space
Gray Aluminum Case with Black
Sport Band

>

Figure 1-8. A user's order history

Account Settings

Account Settings is where you can edit your payment methods and shipping address.

More

There are more features. The Notification settings is the place where you specify whether you want to receive push notifications concerning your order status.

On this screen, you can also access the help page as well as sales and refund policy, privacy olicy, and copyright information.

Cart

Cart (or Bag in the most recent version of the app) is your shopping basket. You can review and edit what's in the cart as well as leave a gift message if you are about to purchase an item for someone else (see Figure 1-9).

G-Tech 1TB G-DRIVE mobile USB 3.0 Hard
Drive (5400 rpm) - Special Edition

$79.95

Delivery:
In Stock

Gift Message
Free

Figure 1-9. An item in a shopping cart

You can also see the subtotal of your purchase and, most important, your payment options (Figure 1-10).

Cart subtotal
Your cart qualifies for free shipping

$79.95

Buy with
other payment options

Buy with Pay

Figure 1-10. Subtotal and payment options in a shopping cart

Note also that the cart icon includes a badge that indicates how many items are in the cart (see Figure 1-11). If your cart is empty, the badge won't show.

Figure 1-11. The badge shows the number of items in your shopping cart

Required Features List

This quick overview of the Apple Store iPhone app provides a good example of the features that an e-commerce app should have. It should:

- List products by categories
- Show a product list for each category
- Show product details
- Have a search feature
- Have a shopping cart
- Show user's favorite (wish list) items
- Show user's order history
- Show company information such as about us, contact us, privacy policy, and copyright information

A good e-commerce app also should enable users to:

- Review products
- Mark a product as a favorite (or add it to a wish list)
- Add a product to a shopping cart
- Create a user account
- Log in and out
- Add and edit a shipping address
- Add and edit a payment method
- Log in with third-party credentials such as Facebook or Twitter
- Request a password reset (in case it slipped their minds)

To run a business, you also need some way to run a marketing campaign:

- Send new product or promotion push notifications to customers
- Ask users to give your app a good review on App Store

To make good business decisions and improve your app, you also need to:

- Track how users use our apps
- Track app crashes

Prerequisites

To develop and publish iOS apps on the App Store, you will need to enroll in the iOS Developer Program and set up a Mac OS development environment on your computer.

iOS Developer Program

By default, the App Store will show the name of the developer enrolled in the iOS Developer Program for each app published under this account. To gain users' trust, however, it's advisable to show the business entity's name instead, as shown in Figure 1-12. To be able to publish an app under the name of a business entity, however, you need to have this D-U-N-S™ number—which is a bit more time consuming than registering with the iOS Developer Program.

Figure 1-12. *Apple publishes the Apple Store app*

Obtaining a D-U-N-S™ number is free. But it can take a month for a US company and even longer if you are not a US company to obtain the number. Once you have the number, it can take up to two weeks for Apple to verify this number. In short, apply for your D-U-N-S earlier rather than later.

> **Note** To learn more about obtaining a D-U-N-S number, go to
> https://developer.apple.com/support/ios/D-U-N-S.php.

Development Environment

To build an iOS app, you also need to have a Mac computer running the latest Mac OS. The development software is Xcode, which includes the iOS SDK (see Figure 1-13).

Figure 1-13. Download Xcode from Mac App Store

Even though you can run sample projects on an iPhone simulator, you really should have an iOS device, such as an iPhone or iPod touch with the latest iOS installed, to ensure your app runs properly on the device.

The sample projects in this book are developed against the latest iOS version, and will always be updated to the latest iOS when it's available.

> **Note**   Apple updates Xcode and the iOS SDK frequently. At the time of writing, I am using Xcode Version 6.3.1 and iOS SDK 8.1.

The Beauty & Me Sample iPhone App

In this book, you learn to build an iOS app for selling beauty and cosmetics products, such as face wash, cleansers, and other skin care products.

As I did with the Apple Store app, I will walk you through most features introduced in the Apple Store app.

> **Note**   To see what the app looks like, you can download it from the App Store by searching "Beauty & Me."

Summary

In this chapter, I gave an overview the Apple Store iPhone app and summarized its features to provide you with some guidelines of what to include in your own e-commerce app.

Chapter 2

Planning and Building the Prototype

Before you start to write the first line of code, it's important to have a mock-up to see what the app looks like, what the user experience is like, what are the features are, and how they are organized. In this chapter, I will show you how to prototype the sample e-commerce iPhone app by using Xcode.

The Apple Store iPhone app uses a UITTabBarController-based user interface (UI) design pattern. This pattern is quite standard and powerful for an e-commerce app; other apps such as Target and EAT24 also use this UI pattern. The good thing about the tab bar interface is that each view controller's state of each tab is automatically persistent. It means that whenever we leave a screen from one tab and play around with other tabs, when we return back to the tab it will always show the content we just left.

This chapter is largely about planning. I won't be giving instructions and showing you figures about how you can drag and drop a UIViewController or a UI Control to UIStoryboard, but in some instances, I will reveal the tricks I have used.

This chapter covers the following:

- User interface and experience
- The proximate total amount of view controllers
- The view controller's type, UITableViewController, or UIViewController
- Custom views
- The appearance of the app

Designing the User Experience

The goal for the sample app that accompanies this book is to present users/customers with an experience that is similar to what they get from the Apple Store iPhone app. The Apple Store app is based on a tabbed design, so you want to use a tapped application template in Xcode. To get started, launch Xcode, and follow these steps:

1. Create a new project based on the Tabbed Application template, and name it, for example, "Chapter 2." In general, the Tabbed Application template is a good fit for an e-commerce mobile app.

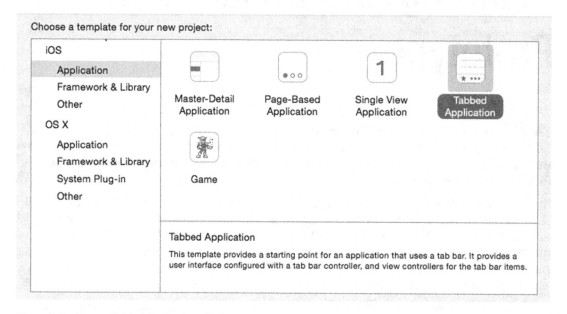

Figure 2-1. *Create a Tabbed Application with Xcode*

2. Next, open the Main.storyboard file. The default nib file is freestyle size. Let's change to iPhone 4-inch on Simulated Metrics, shown in Figure 2-2.

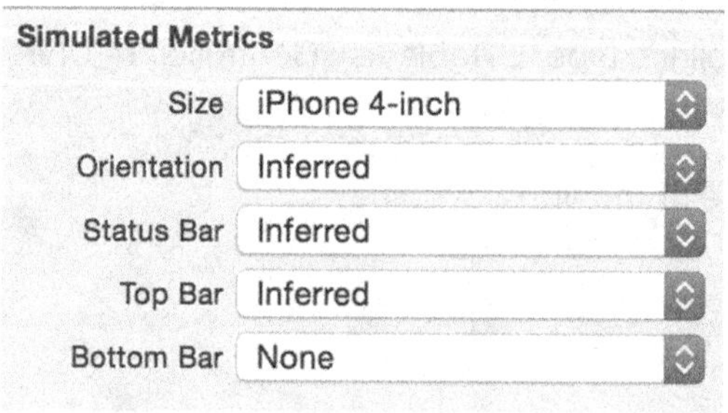

Figure 2-2. *Change Simulated Metrics to iPhone 4-inch*

3. Add three navigation controllers.

4. Holding "control" key, drag the root TabController to the three navigation controllers. A UITabBar shows up on each UINavigationController, as shown in Figure 2-3.

5. Change the title of the three UITabBars to "Shop," "My Account," and "Bag," respectively (see Figure 2-3).

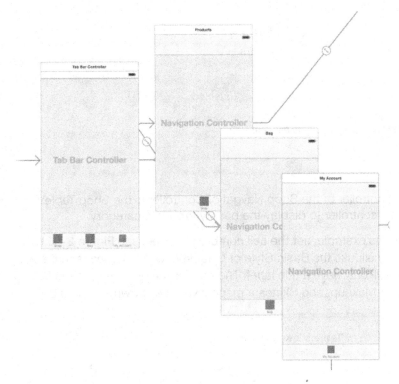

Figure 2-3. Connect the three UINavigationControllers to the TabController

Figure 2-4. Change the name of the Tab bar item

Shop

The root view controller of the Shop NavgationController is the Shop TableViewController. You will use this controller to display the beauty products category.

1. For this example, set the cell numbers to three (see Figure 2-5). For each cell, use the Basic Style of UITableViewCell. It means that each cell will only have a title label. The text for these three labels is Bath & Body, Makeup, and Skincare respectively, as shown in Figure 2-6.

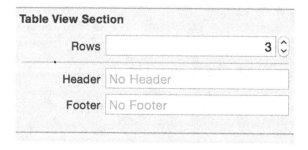

Figure 2-5. Set three static rows for a UITableView

Bath & Body

Makeup

Skincare

Figure 2-6. The is the partial user interface of Shop TableViewController

2. The sample will show a list of products under each product category, so you want to add another UITableViewController to the UIStoryboard. Give it an identifier of ProductsTableViewController and a title of Products, as shown in Figure 2-7.

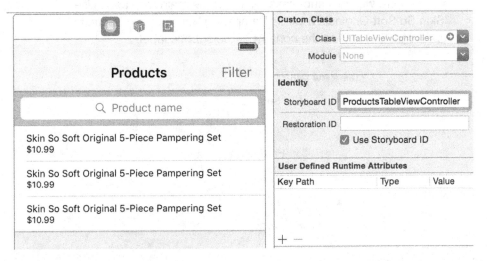

Figure 2-7. Set Identifier for a UITableViewController

3. Next, you want to connect the "Bath & Body" cell of the ShopTableViewController to the ProductsTableViewController. Hold the Control key and drag-and-drop mouse cursor between the cell and the target view controller to connect the two controllers.

4. Build and run the project on an iPhone simulator. When you tap the Bath & Body cell in the first screen of the app, you should see an empty Products table titled Products, as shown in Figure 2-8.

Figure 2-8. This is the user interface of Products UITableViewController

Next, you will work on the Products UITableViewController. The view controller will show information about the product, such as the product name and unit price. You can also add search and filter features to it.

1. For each cell, use the Subtitle style, as shown in Figure 2-9, which means there will be a subtitle label under the main text label. Use "Skin So Soft Originals 5-piece Pampering Set" as the main text label, and "$10.99" as the content of the subtitle label.

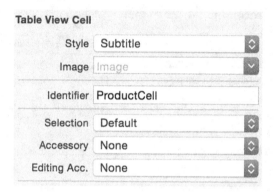

Figure 2-9. *Use "Subtitle" Style for UITableViewCell*

2. Drag a UISearchBar to the ProductsTableViewController, and set the placeholder text to "Product name." See Figure 2-10. This provides a hint to users that search terms entered by them will only search for product names.

Figure 2-10. *Add a UISearchBar to UITableView*

3. In the "Beauty & Me" sample app, the user can filter products based on the price range. Add a UIBarButtonItem to the Products TableViewController and change its title to "Filter." Add a new UIViewController, set "FilterViewController" as its identifier, and set "Price Filter" as the title. Connect the Filter UIBarButtonItem with the new FilterviewController. Presenting the view controller modally is a better user experience. You will also want to add a system Cancel UIBarButtonItem to the left and a system Done UIBarButtonItem to the right of the view controller.

4. In order to let the user quickly change the price range, use two UISlider controls: one is for setting the minimum price; the other is for setting the maximum price. You also need two UILabel controls to show the current minimum UISlider's value and the current maximum of the UISlider's value. Add a few other UILabels to tell users what ranges he can adjust, as shown in Figure 2-11.

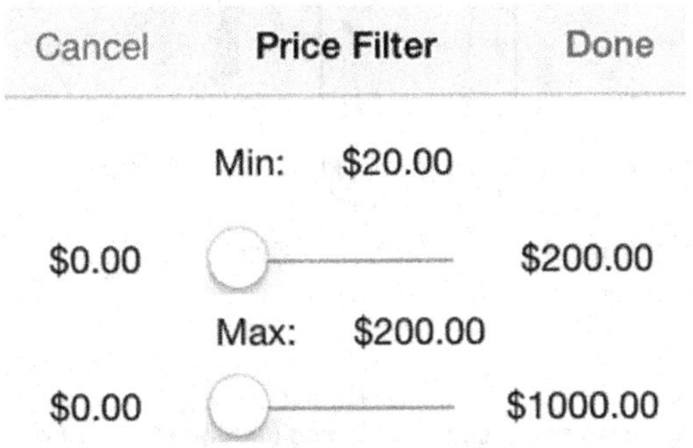

| Cancel | **Price Filter** | Done |

Min: $20.00

$0.00   ⊙———— $200.00

Max: $200.00

$0.00   ⊙———— $1000.00

Figure 2-11. The is the user interface of FilterViewController

5. When a user taps a product cell, the product's detail is displayed, as shown in Figure 2-12. Add a new UIViewController with identifier of "ProductDetailViewController" to the UIStoryboard, and connect any cell on the ProductsTableViewController to the new view controller. The title of the ProductDetailViewController should be the product name you selected, and it needs to be changed based on the user's selection. Right now, let's just put "Skin So Soft Original 5-piece Pampering Set" as its title.

Advanced Repair Recovery Complex II

$ 92.00/ea

Lorem ipsum dolor sit er elit lamet, consectetaur cillium adipisicing pecu, sed do eiusmod tempor incididunt ut l

Add to Bag

Figure 2-12. The is the user interface of ProductDetailViewController

6. The product detail view controller will show a full-size image of the product, product name, price, and description; you also need a button to let a user add the product to her shopping bag. Finally, you want the user to be able to add the product to the favorites list, so add another button with a title "Favorite it."

7. Build the project and run it on the simulator again. Even though you have not added the real search, filter, add-to-bag, and favorite-it functionality, it still gives you some idea what the app will look like. And most important, you can do more about the user interface design.

Figure 2-13 shows the all UIViewControllers for the "Shop" feature.

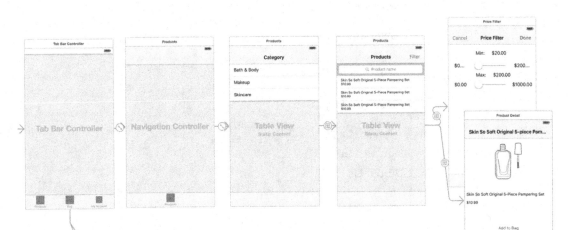

Figure 2-13. This is the view controllers used in Shop

My Account

The root view controller, MyAccountTableViewController, is the place to have all users' activities, such as the shipping and payment address, the order history, and payment methods. We also use this place to show information about the app, privacy policy, contact information, and app version – just like the Apple Store iPhone app.

For the MyAccuntTableViewController, let make its UITableView the Grouped Style, and set three sections. For each cell, we set it as Static and Basic style. Figure 2-14 illustrates what the view controller looks like.

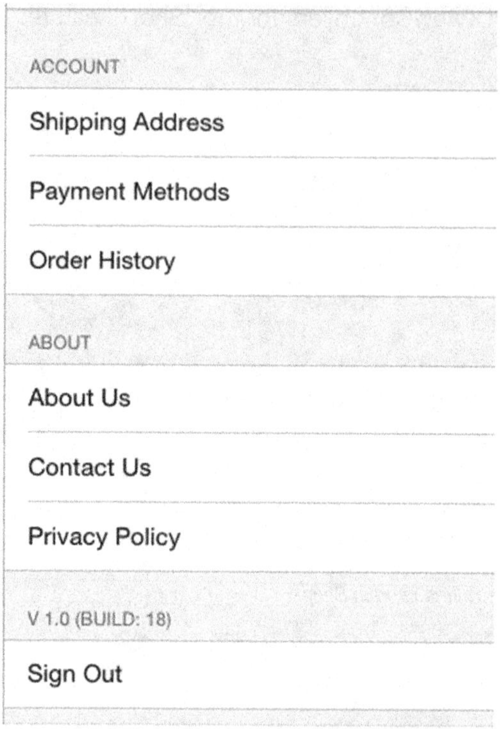

ACCOUNT

Shipping Address

Payment Methods

Order History

ABOUT

About Us

Contact Us

Privacy Policy

V 1.0 (BUILD: 18)

Sign Out

Figure 2-14. Practical user interface of MyAccountTableViewController

The "Sign Out" cell is to log the user out. When the cell is tapped, a screen is displayed to ask the user to log in again. This will involve some programming so we will cover it later.

First, I will focus on prototyping in the first "Account" section.

1. Add another UITableViewController to the main UIStoryboard, use "UserAddressTableViewController" as its identifier, and use "Shipping Address" as its title, as in Figure 2-15.

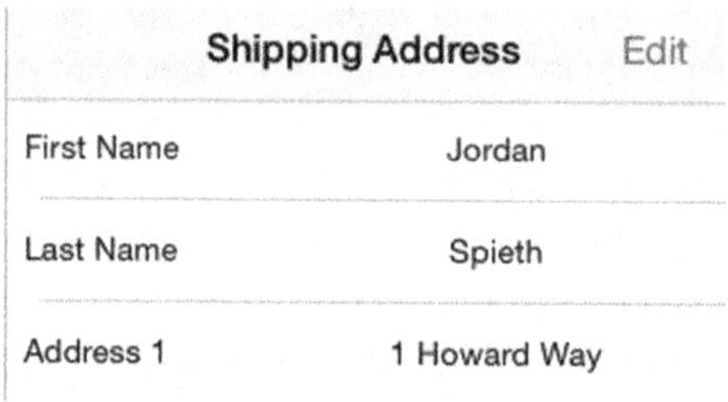

Shipping Address   Edit

First Name   Jordan

Last Name   Spieth

Address 1   1 Howard Way

Figure 2-15. This is part of the user interface of UserAddressTableViewController

2. This time, customize the UserAddressTableViewController's UITableViewCell a bit. Ideally, users should be able to edit their shipping address information. For each cell, use a UILabel to tell what the cell is about, and use a UITextField to take the user's input. On the other hand, a better user experience is to make the UITextField uneditable by default if we know the user has complete address information. Use an Edit system UIBarButtonItem to ask the user to tap the button to edit one's information to avoid editing this information by mistake.

3. Connect the first cell of the first section on "MyAccountTableViewController" to the new "UserAddressTableViewController."

4. Build and run the project; then we should be able to play with the new features.

Next, let's work on the payment methods UI. You technically can't store a user's credit card number or CVC numbers, but you can store a credit card's type such as Visa, Master Card, or American Express; the last four digits; and expiration month and year. Usually a user adds a few credit cards into his account. So you want to use a UITableViewController to show all cards linked to the account.

1. Add a new UITableViewController to your main UIStoryboard, and name it "UserPaymentMethodsTableViewController." For the UITableView, make it Plain style and Static Cells as its Content. You will need one section and two cells.

2. Set each cell as "Subtitle Style." For the first cell, set the content for its TextLabel: Visa XXXX-XXXX-XXXX-4242, 04/20 as the subtitle text; use MasterCard XXXX-XXXX-XXXX-XXXX-4444 and 05/18 for the second cell, as shown in Figure 2-16.

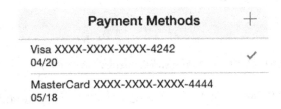

Figure 2-16. Practical user interface of UserPaymentMethodsTableViewController

3. Typically, when a user first signs up for an account with us, there will be no credit card information on file. You should provide a way for the user to add a new card. Drag a UIBarButtonItem to the left bar button item of the view controller, and set it to the system "Add" bar button item.

4. Another use case is that you need to set a default credit card for the user to help speed up the checkout process. Set the first credit card as the default and use a checkmark representing it. But allow the user to set any card as the default.

5. Next, let's prototype a user's order history. Add another UITableViewController to the UIStoryboard, name it "UserOrderHistoryTableViewController" as its identifier, and use "Order History" as the title of the controller.

6. Typically, you will show when the order is placed; a total amount of the purchase; items ordered if there is enough room and an order status; or at a minimum, you need to highlight some canceled orders. First, make the cell height taller, 66. Then put three UILabels on a single cell: one label is for the order date, the other one is for the total amount, and the other one is the product name. For the label, set the number of lines to 0 and the line breaks to Word Wrap. It's pretty common that a user would order multiple products so the product name label won't show all the product's names. Use gray text color to represent a canceled order, as shown in Figure 2-17.

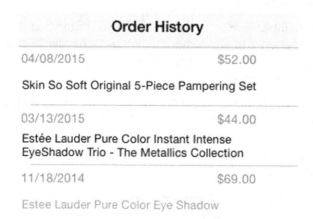

Order History

04/08/2015	$52.00

Skin So Soft Original 5-Piece Pampering Set

03/13/2015	$44.00

Estée Lauder Pure Color Instant Intense
EyeShadow Trio - The Metallics Collection

11/18/2014	$69.00

Estee Lauder Pure Color Eye Shadow

Figure 2-17. This is a partial user interface of UserOrderHistoryTableViewController

This is all you need for "MyAccount." Now you can build the project and run it. Figure 2-18 shows each view controller used in My Account.

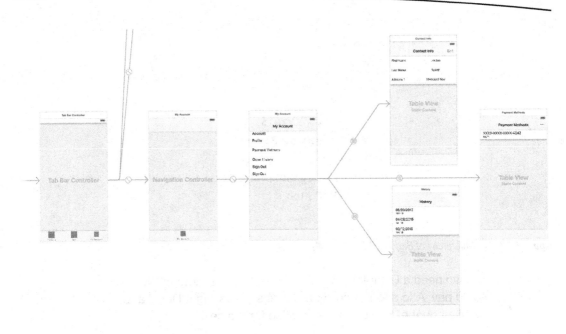

Figure 2-18. Here are the My Account view controllers

Shopping Bag

The root view controller of the BagNavigationController is a UITableViewController. To show what's in the user's bag, use the UITableviewController and name it "BagTableViewController" and "Bag" as its title.

In addition, the following requirements need to be met. The user has to be able to check out; the user should be able to change the quantity of an item or remove an item from the bag; and the bag should show the total amount, which needs to change automatically according to an item's unit price and quantity.

1. First, work on the UITableViewCell. There's quite a lot of content to show so let's make the cell taller. in this example, set it to 66.

2. You also need three UILabels: One is for the product name, the other is for the unit price, and the third is for the quantity. Also add a UIStepper control to the cell so that a user can change the quantity she wants to purchase, as shown in Figure 2-19.

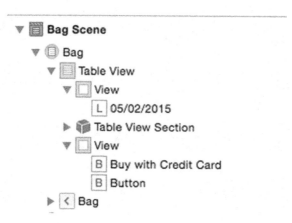

Figure 2-19. *View hierarchy of BagTableViewController*

3. You also need a UITableViewCell to show the total amount the user should pay. Add another cell and set its style as Right Detail and set a total amount of $36.00 as the subtitle for the cell.

4. It's quite common that the user wants to leave an instruction about the order, so add a Compose system UIBarButtonItem to the view controller. It doesn't' really do anything right now, but at least it shows we have this feature in mind.

5. Drag two UIViews: one is for the header view of the UITableView, the other is the footer view.

6. Add a UILabel to the table header view. The UILabel will be used to show when those items have been added into the bag.

7. Add two UIButtons to the footer view. One button has a title "Buy with Credit Card," and the other one is for "Buy with Apple Pay." We need to download the graphic asset for the button from Apple's web site. It comes with our chapter source code. Figure 2-20 illustrates what Bag UITableViewController looks like. Figure 2-21 shows all view controllers for Shopping Bag.

Figure 2-20. *This is the partial user interface of BagTableViewController*

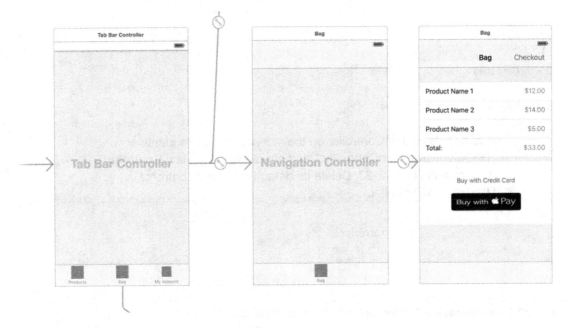

Figure 2-21. *The view controllers used in Shopping Bag*

Sign Up or Log In

A user-friendly app doesn't always require a user to create an account from the beginning. It gives a user the chance to understand what the app is about and what value the app can add to the user's life. Our Beauty & Me is no exception.

For this prototype, ask the user to create an account or log in when one of the following conditions is met. The user taps one of the following:

- "My account" tab
- "Shopping Bag" tab
- "Add To Bag" button on ProductDetailViewController

Let's create another storyboard to handle the login and sign-up work flow.

1. Open the existing project. From the Xcode File menu, select New ➤ File. A dialog window is shown as in Figure. 2-22. Next, choose User Interface and select Storyboard. Name the UIStoryboard LoginSignup.storyboard.

Figure 2-22. Create a UIStoryboard file

2. Add a UINavigationController on the storyboard, set its identifier "DispatchNavigationController," and check "Is Initial View Controller", as shown in Figure 2-23. Delete its default root view controller, a UITableViewController.

View Controller

Title

☑ Is Initial View Controller

Figure 2-23. Set the DispatchNavigationController as an initial View Controller

3. Add a UIViewController, and set it to the root view controller of the DispatchNavigationController. Name the new root view controller with an identifier of "DispatchViewController" and set "Beauty & Me" as its title.

4. Add three buttons on the view of the DispatchViewController, and give the title for each button—"Log In with Facebook," "Sign Up," and "Log In," respectively. The reason you want to put the "Log In with Facebook" button on top is that you really want to encourage users to create an account with us.

5. The DispatchNavigationController will be presented modally so a user will have a chance to cancel the process. Add a system cancel UIBarButtonItem to the left of the UIBarButtonItem.

This feature will only work once you have implemented what happens when a user taps the "Log In with Facebook" button. Right now, it won't do anything.

6. Add another UIViewController, and name it "SignUpViewController" with "Sign Up" as the title. Connect the "Sign Up" button with the SignUpViewController. On the view controller, let a user enter his or her e-mail and password to sign up for an account with you. To make sure the user can remember his password, let the user enter his or her password one more time. A standard way to create the user experience is to use a UITableView with three cells. Use each cell to hold a UITextField. Put a placeholder text on each UITextField to indicate what the cell is for, as seen in Figure. 2-24. Add a UIButton with the title "Sign Up" under the UITableView, and add a UIBarButtonItem with a title "Sign Up" to the right bar button item so a user can tap either one to sign up.

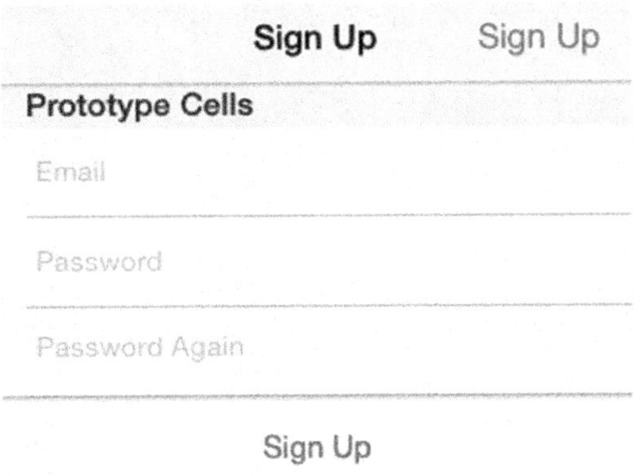

Figure 2-24. This is a partial user interface of SignupViewController

7. In similar fashion, add another UIViewController, and name it "LoginViewController" with a title "Log In." Add a UITableView with two static cells. This time you only need the user's e-mail and password to log in with you. Figure 2-25 shows what it looks like.

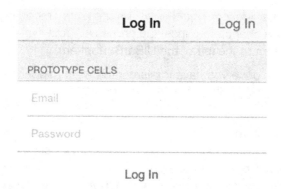

Figure 2-25. *This is a partial user interface of LoginViewController*

Figure 2-26 shows the whole LoginSignup.storyboard

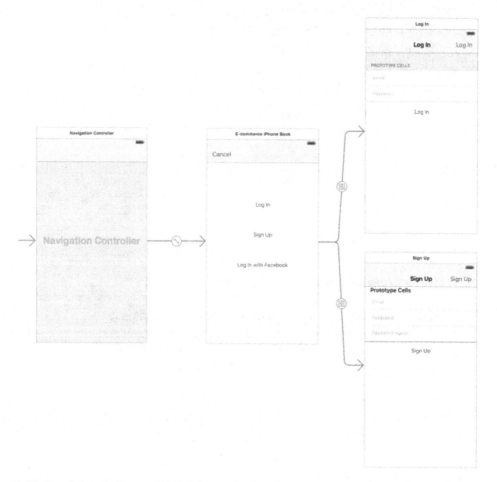

Figure 2-26. *The view controllers used in LoginSignup.storyboard*

Put It All Together

To make our prototype work like the real thing, you need to write a little bit of code to handle cases:

- A user has not created an account but tapped "My Account" or "Add to Bag."

- A user logs out.

You may wonder whether you can ask a user to register an account with you when he/she just opens the app? Technically, yes, you can, but it's not a good user experience. A user doesn't know what the app is and what it can do, and you already ask him or her to register an account? Most likely the user will quit and delete the app.

Use NSUserDefault to save the login/logout status of a customer. When the app just opens, assume the user is not a registered user. Here is the code:

AppDelegate.m

```
- (BOOL)application:(UIApplication *)application didFinishLaunchingWithOptions:
(NSDictionary *)launchOptions {
    // Override point for customization after application launch.
    UITabBarController *tabBarController = (UITabBarController*)self.window.
    rootViewController;
    tabBarController.delegate = self;

     NSString *const kIsLoggedInfKey   = @"kIsLoggedIn";

    [[NSUserDefaults standardUserDefaults] registerDefaults:@{kIsLoggedInfKey:@(NO)}];
    return YES;
}
```

When the user taps "My Account" or "Shopping Bag" tab, show our DispatchViewController. To do this, you need to a little bit more work.

First, In AppDelegate, you need to declare UITabBarContollerDelegate:

```
UITabBarController *tabBarController = (UITabBarController*)self.window.rootViewController;
    tabBarController.delegate = self;
```

When the user taps a tab other than "My Account" or "Shopping Bag," don't ask the user to sign up or log in.

Here is how to implement one of UITabBarControllerDelegates to respond to a tab selected:

```
- (void)tabBarController:(UITabBarController *)tabBarController didSelectViewController:
(UIViewController *)viewController{
    UINavigationController *navViewController = (UINavigationController *)viewController;
    if (![navViewController.title isEqualToString:@"Shop"]) {
        if (!([[NSUserDefaults standardUserDefaults] boolForKey:kIsLoggedInfKey])) {
            UIStoryboard *dispatchStoryboard = [UIStoryboard storyboardWithName:
            @"LoginSignup" bundle:nil];
```

```
                UINavigationController *navController = (UINavigationController *)
                [dispatchStoryboard instantiateInitialViewController];
                [self.window.rootViewController presentViewController:navController
                animated:YES completion:nil];
            }
        }
    }
```

First, check which tap is selected by checking the title of navigation controllers. Then ask whether the user is logged in or not; If not, grab the Dispatch navigation controller by its storyboard identifier, then present it.

In Dispatch view controller, implement two IBActions: A user logs in by using the "Log In with Facebook" feature, or a user cancels the login or sign-up process:

```
-(IBAction)onFacebookLogin:(id)sender{
    [[NSUserDefaults standardUserDefaults] setBool:YES forKey:kIsLoggedInfKey];
    [[NSUserDefaults standardUserDefaults] synchronize];
    [self dismissViewControllerAnimated:YES completion:nil];
}
```

Here you simply set the kIsLoggedInKey of NSUserDefaults to Yes then dismiss the Dispatch navigation view controller.

```
-(IBAction)onCancel:(id)sender{
    [self dismissViewControllerAnimated:YES completion:nil];
}
```

Once the user taps the "Cancel" UIBarButtonItem, we dismiss the Dispatch navigation view controller.

> **Note**   A complete implementation can be found in the Chapter 2 source code.

Summary

In this chapter, I cover how to use UIStoryboard to create the prototype for the app used in this book. I have used the Tabbed Application template. Three tabs, namely, "Shop", "Shopping Bag," and "My Account" lead to three different main features for the app. I also showed how to set up a sign-up or login UIStoryboard. With some code to fake a signed-in user, I created a prototype of the app.

Chapter **3**

Parse Fundamentals

Parse has numerous features and functionality to help make a developer's life easier. These features are covered throughout the book. This chapter focuses on the Parse iOS SDK.

In this chapter you learn about:

- Interacting with the Parse PFObject class and subclasses
- Retrieving data with the PFQuery class
- Creating relations between objects with pointers, arrays, Parse relations, and joining tables
- Loading and displaying images with the PFImageView class
- Displaying images with the PFTableViewCell class
- Querying and showing data with the PFQueryTableViewController class

Interacting with Objects: PFObject

If you're an iOS developer, you are familiar with NSObject. NSObject is the root class of most Objective-C class hierarchies. PFObject is the root Parse iOS class. When developing an iOS app, you start with PFObject:

```
@interface PFObject : NSObject
```

What makes PFObject so easy to work with Parse's back end is that each PFObject contains key/value pairs of JSON-compatible data. This data is *schemaless*, which means that you don't need to specify ahead of time what keys exist on each PFObject—you simply set whatever key/value pairs you want, and Parse's back end will store it.

Another nice feature is that Parse doesn't limit how a new class is created. You go to your project home on the Parse web site, and add a new class from the Data browser, by importing data, or from a client. To create a new class from a client, remember to turn on client class creation in the settings page of your project home (see Figure 3-1).

Figure 3-1. *Enable "Allow client class creation" in the Parse console*

For example, to create a Product class with properties such as title, subtitle, unit price, and price per unit (each, lbs, etc.), write the following code in Xcode:

```
PFObject *product = [PFObject objectWithClassName:@"Product"];
[product setObject:@"iOS eCommerce App Development with Parse" forKey:@"title"];
[product setObject:@(19.99) forKey:@"unitPrice"];
[product setObject:@"ea" forKey:@"priceUnit"];
[product setObject:@"A real world iOS app development with Parse" forKey:@"subtitle"];
[product save];
```

To save the class, you call a PFObject save method. If there is no class called "Product" on the Parse back end, Parse will create one for you. In the meantime, add a row of data for this class, as shown in Figure 3-2.

Figure 3-2. *Parse created a Product class with a row of records*

If a class called "Product" already exists on the back end, executing the same code will add another row of data.

Although creating classes is easy, you can run into problems quickly. For example, each class object has little to do with the real business object you try to mimic. In this case, the Product is the real object you want to represent, but you only call it PFObject, not Product. Also, you have to remember all keys and set those keys with the proper values; it's kind of like working with NSDictionary. Luckily, the Parse native PFObject subclass comes to the rescue.

Working with PFObject subclassing is even easier than working with classes. Here is how. In Xcode, create a new file and select Cocoa Touch Class; then name the file Product and make it a subclass of PFObject, as shown in Figure 3-3.

Class:	Product
Subclass of:	PFObject

Figure 3-3. *Create a Product subclass of PFObject with Xcode*

This creates two files: Product.h and Product.m.

In Product.h, you need to declare that the Product class needs to conform to the PFSubclassing protocol; then, create an NSObject with title, subtitle, unit price, and price unit properties as usual.

```
#import <Parse/Parse.h>
@interface Product : PFObject<PFSubclassing>
@property (nonatomic, copy) NSString *title;
@property (nonatomic, copy) NSString *subtitle;
@property (nonatomic, assign) double unitPrice;
@property (nonatomic, copy) NSString *priceUnit;
@end
```

In Product.m, you need to import <Parse/PFSubclassing.h>:

```
#import "Product.h"
#import <Parse/PFObject+Subclass.h>
```

For this implementation, use the @dynamic keyword for your properties:

```
@dynamic title, subtitle, priceUnit, unitPrice;
And there is another required method to implement
+(NSString *)parseClassName
{
    return @"Product";
}
```

That's it. Here is the complete code for the Product.m file:

```
#import "Product.h"
#import <Parse/PFObject+Subclass.h>
@implementation Product
@dynamic title, subtitle, priceUnit, unitPrice;

+(NSString *)parseClassName
{
    return @"Product";
}
@end
```

There is one more thing you need to do. In the AppDelegate.m file, declare the Product class before declaring anything else Parse related:

```
#import "AppDelegate.h"
#import <Parse/Parse.h>
#import "Product.h"

@implementation AppDelegate
- (BOOL)application:(UIApplication *)application didFinishLaunchingWithOptions:
(NSDictionary *)launchOptions {
    [Product registerSubclass];
```

```
[Parse setApplicationId:@"YOUR-PARSE-APPLICATION-ID"   clientKey:@"YOUR-PARSE-CLIENT-
KEY"];
    return YES;
}
```

Basically, this is how you create a PFObject subclass. Using the Product class is now much easier and intuitive:

```
Product *product = [Product object];
product.title = @"iOS eCommerce App Development with Parse";
product.subtitle = @"A real world iOS app development with Parse";
product.priceUnit = @"ea";
product.unitPrice = 19.99;
[product save];
```

Working with an object constantly involves four types of action queries: create, read, update, and delete. Parse makes it easier for developers with its subclasses. Take the following Product subclass uses cases, for example.

Create—As you have seen, it's easy to create a product object instance:

```
Product *product = [Product object];
```

Read—Read properties of a product object can be done as usual, using the standard way to work with NSObject. For example, if you want to print the product's title to the console, use:

```
NSLog(@"%@", product.title);
```

Edit—Editing a product could mean changing the properties of a product, say, setting a new price for this product:

```
product.unitPrice = 21.99;
```

It is very important to save the updated product into Parse, so you call:

```
[product save];
```

Alternatively, you can also call the save method asynchronously—always the recommended approach for a better user experience:

```
[product saveInBackground];
```

Delete—Like an NSObject instance, set this object to nil. However, you also need to let Parse know this object no longer exists, so call the delete method:

```
[product delete];
```

Or call it asynchronously:

```
[product deleteInBackground];
```

> **Note**   For more information about PFObject and its APIs, got to
> https://parse.com/docs/ios/api/Classes/PFObject.html.

Retrieving Data: PFQuery

Since all of your data is stored on Parse, getting the data out of Parse is important. To do so, you query Parse using the PFQuery helper class.

PFQuery is a subclass of PFObject, and it makes the common query-related API calls easier. Say you want to create a PFQuery instance, you can use:

```
PFQuery *query = [PFQuery queryWithClassName:@"Product"];
```

The built-in class method (+PFQuery *)queryWithClassName with a parameter of the class name indicates that the Product class is queried.

Parse provides many easy-to-remember and easy-to-use methods to help keep the query developer friendly.

Say, you want to retrieve all of your products, you can use:

```
NSArray *products = [query findObjects];
```

Or you can use an asynchronous method:

```
__block NSArray *products;
[query findObjectsInBackgroundWithBlock:^(NSArray *objects, NSError *error){
        if (!error) {
            products = objects;
        }
 }];
```

By default, Parse will return the first 200 items of products stored on Parse. If you want to customize the number of items retrieved, use the PFQuery method: -(void)setLimit: (NSInteger)limit

```
[query setLimit:100];
```

If you only want to get a product with the title of "iOS eCommerce App Development with Parse," use query constraint methods:

```
[query whereKey:@"title" equalTo:@"iOS eCommerce App Development with Parse"];
```

You can also customize the sort order of your returned objects. The default result is sorted with the createdAt property in ascending order. If you want to sort the returned items alphabetically by product title and in ascending order, use this:

```
[query orderByAscending:@"title"];
```

Combining those constraints, you can perform very powerful queries.

> **Note**   For more information about PFQuery and its APIs, go to
> `https://parse.com/docs/ios/api/Classes/PFQuery.html`.

Creating Relations between Objects

Objects can have multiple relationships with other objects. A product normally belongs to a product category. This book is normally put in the Computer Programming category in Barnes & Noble. The Computer Programming category has many different programming books: a typical one-to-many relationship scenario.

Probably you have heard of other relationship types such as one-to-one and many-to-many. Parse provides four different ways to build relationships: pointers, arrays, Parse relations, and joining tables.

Using Pointers

Pointers are used for one-to-one and one-to-many relationships. For example, suppose you have a book and book category with a Product class and a ProductCategory class; this is how you can define the relationship using the PFObject subclasses in Product.h:

```
#import <Parse/Parse.h>
@class ProductCategory;
@interface Product : PFObject<PFSubclassing>
@property (nonatomic, copy) NSString *title;
@property (nonatomic, copy) NSString *subtitle;
@property (nonatomic, assign) double unitPrice;
@property (nonatomic, copy) NSString *priceUnit;
@property (nonatomic, strong) ProductCategory *category;
@end
```

Say you have a Product Category object with title "Programming Books," and you want the book to belong to this category, use this:

```
ProductCategory *category = [ProductCategory object];
category.title = @"Programming Book";

Product *product = [Product object];
product.category = category;
[product saveInBackground];
```

The nice thing about Parse is that if you save this product now, the category object of ProductCategory will automatically be saved to Parse without explicitly calling a save method.

Once you have built the one-to-many relationship between this book and the book category, and you want to show all books in the programming book category, use this query:

```
PFQuery *query = [PFQuery queryWithClassName:@"Product"];
[query whereKey:@"category" equalTo:category];
 [query findObjectsInBackgroundWithBlock:^(NSArray *objects, NSError *error){
        if (!error) {


        }
}];
```

> **Note**   If you have a few custom query methods, it's better to put them in the subclass instead of in the main view controller you will work with.

Using Arrays

Arrays are used in many-to-many relationships in much the same way that they are for one-to-many relationships. All objects on one side of the relationship will have an Array column containing several objects on the other side of the relationship. In the case of a book product, several authors can write a book. This is how to declare this relationship in the Product class:

```
#import <Parse/Parse.h>
@class ProductCategory;
@interface Product : PFObject<PFSubclassing>
@property (nonatomic, copy) NSString *title;
@property (nonatomic, copy) NSString *subtitle;
@property (nonatomic, assign) double unitPrice;
@property (nonatomic, copy) NSString *priceUnit;
@property (nonatomic, strong) ProductCategory *category;
@property (nonatomic, strong) NSArray *authors;
@end
```

Suppose you have two Author objects:

```
product.authors = @[author1, author2];
```

When performing a Product query, if you also want to get the related authors, use a -(void) include PFQuery method. The following code shows how you can get all authors from a Product query, and print the first author's name:

```
PFQuery *query = [PFQuery queryWithClassName:@"Product"];
[query includeKey:@"authors"];
[query findObjectsInBackgroundWithBlock:^(NSArray *objects, NSError *error){
        if (!error) {
            Product *product = objects[0];
            NSArray *authors = product.authors;
            PFUser *author = authors[0];
            NSLog(@"%@", [author objectForKey:@"name"]);
        }
}];
```

> **Note** It's important to use the `includeKey` method when you want to get the object data that the array contains.

Using Parse Relations

Parse relations, or PFRelation, works similarly to an NSArray of PFObjects. The difference is that you don't need to download all the objects in a relation at once. This allows PFRelation to scale many more objects than the NSArray of the PFObject approach. One example is that a user may like many products. To save the products the user has liked, you can use PFRelation:

```
PFObject *user = [PFObject object];
PFRelation *relation = [user relationForKey:@"likes"];
[relation addObject:product];
[user saveInBackground];
```

To remove a product from the user's favorites list, use:

```
[relation removeObject:product];
```

By default, the list of products that the user has collected is not downloaded. You can get the list of products in this way:

```
[[relation query] findObjectsInBackgroundWithBlock:^(NSArray *objects, NSError *error){
        if (!error) {
            Product *product = objects[0];
            NSLog(@"%@", product.title);
        }
 }];
```

Joining Tables

Using the join tables method helps you get more information besides the relationship. Take the following use case, for example: if you want to build a relationship between a user and the product he reviewed, you care about who writes the review, which product is reviewed, and the review content. The ProductReview PFObject subclass for this use case looks like this:

```
#import <Parse/Parse.h>
@class Product;
@interface ProductReview : PFObject
@property (nonatomic, strong) PFUser *user;
@property (nonatomic, strong) Product *product;
@property (nonatomic, copy) NSString *content;
@end
```

Introducing a Special Parse Object: PFUser

The PFUser class is a local representation of a user persisted to the Parse Data. This class is a subclass of a PFObject and has all the same features, such as flexible schema, automatic persistence, and a key value interface. The difference is that PFUser has some special additions specific to user accounts, including authentication, sign up, and validation uniqueness.

Notably, username and password are two required properties for PFUser. The e-mail property of PFUser is always there even though you might want to set a value for it.

To sign up a user with a username and password, start by creating a PFUser instance:

```
PFUser *user = [PFUser user];
```

Next, get the username and password from two UITextField instances:

```
user.username =usernameTextField.text;
user.password = passwordTextField.text;
```

Then call the -(BOOL)signUp method, or asynchronically the signUp method,

```
[user signUpInBackgroundWithBlock:^(BOOL succeeded, NSError *error){
        if (!error){


        }
}];
```

It is quite common nowadays to require a user's e-mail address as username. You can use a UITextField to collect the user's e-mail:

```
user.username = emailTextField.text;
user.password = passwordTextField.text;
user.email = emailTextField.text;
```

Next, you need to verify the text in emailTextField is a valid e-mail address. Parse provides the emailVerified property for PFUser. The value of emailVerified can only be set to true while this user clicks a link in the verification e-mail sent by Parse (this process is discussed in Chapter 19).

You log in a user with the PFUser class method logInWithUsernameInBackground:password:

```
[PFUser logInWithUsernameInBackground:emailTextField.text password:passwordTextField.text
block:^(PFUser *user, NSError *error){
        if (!error) {


        }
}];
```

Once this user has logged in, use the class method [PFUser currentUser] to get an instance of the current user. The user is persisted on the client. Unless the user has logged out, you can always use this method to get the current user.

To log the user out, simply call this method:

```
[PFUser logOut];
```

Parse also provides an Anonymous Users feature. An anonymous user can be created without a username and password while still retaining all of the same capabilities as any other PFUser. After logging out, an anonymous user is abandoned, and the user's data is no longer accessible. A typical use case is to create an anonymous user when your app is launched for the first time; you then let the user add products to the shopping bag, and keep track of what the user has liked. You won't ask the user to sign up with an e-mail and password until later or the user's data will be discarded.

To enable this feature, call it in `application:didFinishLaunchingWithOptions:` in AppDelegate.m:

```
[PFUser enableAutomaticUser];
```

Once this method is called, when check [PFUser currentUser], it won't return a nil.

To check whether the current user is an anonymous user, use the PFAnonymousUtils method + (BOOL)isLinkedWithUser:(nullable PFUser *)user:

```
if ([PFAnonymousUtils isLinkedWithUser:[PFUser currentUser]]){
        NSLog(@"It is an anonymous user.");
}
```

You can create a subclass of PFUser the same way you created a PFObject subclass. For example, if you have a Customer object, the Customer.h file will look like this:

```
#import <Parse/Parse.h>
@interface Customer : PFUser<PFSubclassing>
@property (nonatomic, copy) NSString *firstName;
@property (nonatomic, copy) NSString *lastName;
@property (nonatomic, copy) NSString *address1;
@property (nonatomic, copy) NSString *city;
@property (nonatomic, copy) NSString *state;
@property (nonatomic, copy) NSString *zipcode;
@end
```

Customer.m will look like this:

```
#import "Customer.h"
#import <Parse/PFObject+Subclass.h>
@implementation Customer
@dynamic firstName, lastName, address1, city, state, zipcode;
@end
```

The +(NSString *)parseClassName method is not required to implement for the subclass of PFUser because the Parse class name will always be "_User."

> **Note** To read more about PFUser, visit `https://parse.com/docs/osx/api/Classes/PFUser.html`.

Loading and Displaying Images: PFImageView

PFImageView is a subclass of UIImageView. It is a helper class that makes downloading image files from the Parse server easier. You use it the same way you use UIImageView. To display an image, write the following:

```
PFImageView *imageView = [[PFImageView alloc] initWithFrame:CGRectMake(0.0, 0.0,
320.0, 180.0)];
imageView.contentMode = UIViewContentModeScaleAspectFill;
imageView.file = product.image;
[imageView loadInBackground];
```

PFImageview has a file property that is an instance of PFFile. Your Product instance has a property image, which is also the instance of PFFile.

> **Note** You can read more about PFFile at `https://parse.com/docs/osx/api/Classes/PFFile.html`.

Displaying an Image in a Cell: PFTableViewCell

PFTableViewCell is a subclass of UITableViewCell. It is a helper class to display any image downloaded from the Parse server more easily.

```
-(PFTableViewCell *)tableView:(UITableView * __nonnull)tableView cellForRowAtIndexPath:
(NSIndexPath * __nonnull)indexPath object:(nullable Product *)object
{
    PFTableViewCell *cell = [tableView dequeueReusableCellWithIdentifier:@"ProductCell"];
    cell.imageView.file = object.image;
    [cell.imageView loadInBackground];
    return cell;
}
```

Querying and Showing Data: PFQueryTableViewController

When you develop an iOS application, you commony use UITableViewController. In a typical network-based app, you use UITableViewController to display the content that is fetched from a remote server. Often you also need to implement some features such as a loading indicator, pull-to-refresh, pagination, tap a cell to load and show next page, and load and show an image on each UITableViewCell. Parse creates this PFQueryTableViewController, a subclass of UITableViewController, to make a developer's life even easier.

Here is an example of how you could use PFQueryTableViewController; let's say you want to implement a feature that shows all products and name it ProductsTableViewController class, as shown in Figure 3-4.

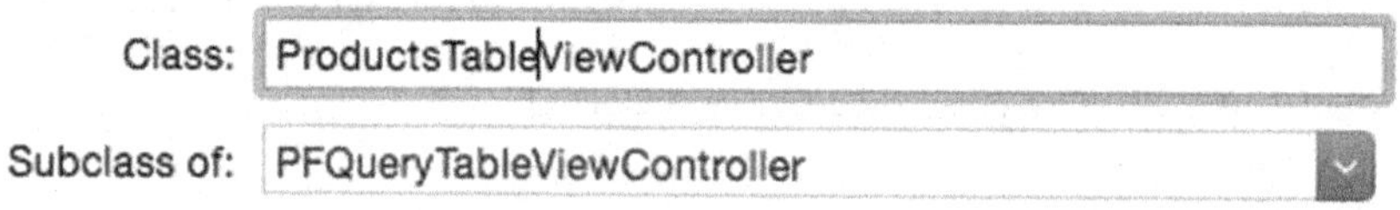

Class:	ProductsTableViewController
Subclass of:	PFQueryTableViewController

Figure 3-4. *Create a PFQueryTableViewController subclass*

This is what ProductsTableViewController.h looks like:

```
#import "PFQueryTableViewController.h"

@interface ProductsTableViewController : PFQueryTableViewController

@end
```

This is what the ProductsTableViewControllerm looks like:

```
#import "ProductsTableViewController.h"
#import "Product.h"
#import <ParseUI/PFTableViewCell.h>
#import <ParseUI/PFImageView.h>
@implementation ProductsTableViewController
-(void)awakeFromNib
{
    [super awakeFromNib];
    self.parseClassName = @"Product";
    self.pullToRefreshEnabled = YES;
    self.paginationEnabled = YES;
    self.objectsPerPage = 10;
}
```

```
- (PFQuery *)queryForTable {
    PFQuery *query = [PFQuery queryWithClassName:self.parseClassName];
    if ([self.objects count] == 0) {
        query.cachePolicy = kPFCachePolicyCacheThenNetwork;
    }
    return query;
}

#pragma mark
-(PFTableViewCell *)tableView:(UITableView * __nonnull)tableView cellForRowAtIndexPath:
(NSIndexPath * __nonnull)indexPath object:(nullable Product *)object
{
    PFTableViewCell *cell = [tableView dequeueReusableCellWithIdentifier:@"ProductCell"];
    cell.textLabel.text = object.title;
        cell.imageView.file = object.image;
    [cell.imageView loadInBackground];
    return cell;
}
@end
```

First, you implement the -(void)awakeFromNib method if you are using the XIB file in a UIStoryboard or a separate XIB file for the ProductsTableViewController. Specify the Parse class name you will use for this controller: in this case, Product class. If you want to use the pull-to-fresh or pagination features, set self.pullToRefreshEnabled and self.paginationEnabled to YES. Also set 10 objects for each page. Depending on the cell height, you can set your number to provide a better user experience.

The second method you need to implement is +(PFQuery *)queryForTable. Specify what Parse class you will query, and the cache policy. In this case, query the Product Parse class and for your cache policy use kPFCachePolicyCacheThenNetwork.

The third method is to display your objects on each PFTableViewCell. In this example, set the product title to the cell's textLabel and the product image to the cell's imageView.

Summary

In this chapter, I have gone over the Parse fundamentals related to building an e-commerce iOS app. I started with the PFObject class and its subclasses, and then introduced four types of relationships in PFObjects and PFUser. I also covered three basic Parse UIs, namely, PFImageView, PFTableViewCell, and PFQueryTableViewController.

Chapter 4

Parse Project Setup

This chapter covers how to set up a Parse project. You will need to write down a few application keys and secrets. To make the process simple, start with a helper class to remember these keys and secrets.

In this chapter you learn how to:

- Keep track of your keys with the EMABConstants helper class
- Create a new Parse app
- Set up payment, transactional e-mails, and Facebook login
- Manage dependencies with Cocoapods
- Implement a progress indicator with SVProgressHud

Keep Track of Your Keys: EMABConstants Class

Continue with the source code from Chapter 2; create a new Cocoa Touch Class file, name it EMABConstants, and make it a subclass of NSObject. One purpose of this class is to keep track of those global accessible NSStrings, such as all keys and secrets. In this case, using "extern NSString *const" is the preferred approach.

In addition, you used EMAB as prefix for each file you created—EMAB stands for "E-commerce Mobile App Development," but you can name it whatever you want.

Create a New Parse App

If you don't have a Parse account, now is the time to sign up for one! Open https://parse.com in your favorite browser, then follow the onscreen instructions to sign up for a Parse account. The process is simple. Once you verify the e-mail address you are asked to provide, you can jump right in to create a new app.

Parse only asks for the name of the new app you want to create. In this tutorial, your app name is EcommerceAppBook. Once you confirm the project name, you will see a project overview similar to the one shown in Figure 4-1.

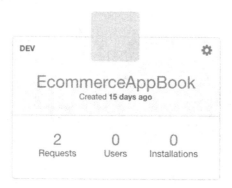

Figure 4-1. *A new Parse app*

Click the icon part of the summary box, and you will then see a dashboard screen. At this point, you only need to get your application keys. So click the "Settings" tab, which is on top of the dashboard, then click "Keys" in the left column. You will see a couple of application keys: Application ID and Client Key for your iOS app (see Figure 4-2).

Application Keys		
Application ID ⑦	74ahhmaQqgos1TFCvVCSAjkaLv6ILY4CCPHDIoXh	Copy
Client Key ⑦	KdP1WZIw1PE0SaRVTL6JPFIFenTNNcRSP4v9BQ5a	Copy

Figure 4-2. *Parse application keys*

Paste these two keys into your EMABConstants.h file:

```
extern NSString *const kParseApplicationID;
extern NSString *const kParseClientKey;
```

In EMABConstants.m, implement these two keys' content:

```
NSString *const kParseApplicationID = @"YOUR-PARSE-APPLICATION-ID";
NSString *const kParseClientKey = @"YOUR-PARSE-CLIENT-KEY";
```

Remember to use your real Parse application ID and client key.

Set Up Payment: Stripe

Wikipedia says that Stripe is a company that provides a way for individuals and businesses to accept payments over the Internet. Stripe says about itself: web and mobile payments, built for developers. The most important feature of an e-commerce app is that it accepts payment. In this tutorial, after a user enters a credit card number, you will use Stripe to process the payment. In the end, Stripe will charge the user's credit card and distribute the money to your bank account, minus a small fee for the service. The amount of the fee is calculated based on your geolocation. For example, at the time of writing, the fee in the United States is 2.4% + 20 cents per successful charge. There are no recurring monthly fees, no refund costs, and no hidden fees. If you haven't done so already, this would be a good time to sign up with Stripe.

> **Note**   For more information about Stripe's pricing, go to `https://stripe.com/gb/pricing`.

To get started with Stripe, click the Sign Up button on the Stripe home page, `https://stripe.com/gb`. As with most accounts these days, you will be asked to provide an e-mail address and a password. Stripe will send you a verification e-mail to the e-mail address you provided. Be sure to verify your e-mail before you continue.

Clicking the link in the verification e-mail will bring you back to the Stripe website. Log in with the e-mail and password to activate your account.

Stripe supports multiple accounts within the same user account. From the Your Account menu, select "Create New Account," and give it an account name, such as your company's name, then click "Create Account," as shown in Figure 4-3.

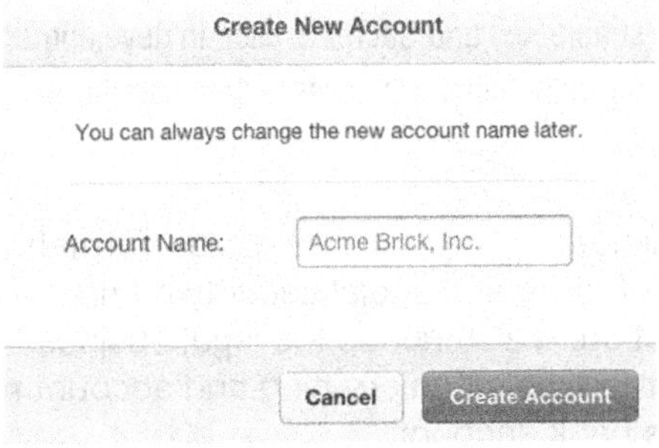

Create New Account

You can always change the new account name later.

Account Name: Acme Brick, Inc.

Cancel   Create Account

Figure 4-3.   Create a new Stripe account

Similar to Parse, you will see a dashboard. Click your account name located at the top right corner, and click "Account Settings" (see Figure 4-4).

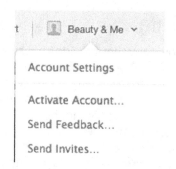

Figure 4-4. Go to Account Settings

Find the "API Keys" tap, and copy and paste the Test Publishable Key and Live Publishable Key to your EMBAConstants class.

In EMABConstants.h:

```
extern NSString *const kStripeTestPublishableKey;
extern NSString *const kStripeLivePublishableKey;
```

In EMABConstants.m:

```
NSString *const kStripeTestPublishableKey = @"YOUR-STRIPE-TEST-PUBLISHABLE-KEY";
NSString *const kStripeLivePublishableKey = @"YOUR-STRIPE-LIVE-PUBLISHABLE-KEY";
```

You won't need the Test Secret Key and Live Secret Key in your Xcode project; however, you will need them later on. The Live Secret Key is very important, and you should not share it with others.

Note   The pair of Test Publishable Key and Secret is used in development; you will need the Live Publishable Key and Secret in production. I will cover how to use the Secret keys in Chapter 14.

Worth mentioning, Stripe will need you to provide more information such as the legal representative's name, date of birth, and social security number for this account when you turn your project into production. It also needs the legal business name, address, and EIN/Tax ID if there is one. And it requires a bank routing and account number so the money can be transferred into the user's bank account.

Set Up Transactional E-Mails: Mailgun

For this example, you will use the developer-friendly Mailgun APIs to send transactional e-mails when an order is placed. Mailgun's pricing is very reasonable The first 10,000 e-mails of the month are free. Alernatively, you can also choose Sendgrid or other services. I chose Mailgun mainly because Parse has a built-in Mailgun cloud module for developers.

> **Note**   For more information about Mailgun's pricing go to `http://www.mailgun.com/pricing`.

Signing up for a Mailgun account is simple. Visit `https://mailgun.com/signup`, and enter your Company/Account name, personal name, e-mail address and password, and sign up.

Mailgun also requires e-mail verification. Follow the verification e-mail instructions, and you will be brought back to the Mailgun website. Log in with your e-mail and password, and you will be sent to a dashboard screen. Tap the "Domains" tab at the top. You will see a default sandbox domain automatically assigned to you; use this domain in your project. Click this domain to find out the API key (see Figure 4-5).

Figure 4-5. The Domains tab in Mailgun

You won't need this API key in your Xcode project; but you will use it later in your Parse Cloud code.

> **Note**   In production, you should set your own e-mail domain with Mailgun so every e-mail sent will be seen from your company's e-mail address.

Set Up Facebook Login

Since you will use the Facebook Login feature, it's mandatory to create a Facebook App with Facebook to enable this feature.

Go to `https://developers.facebook.com/apps`. Click "Add a New App," and choose iOS. You will see a "Quick Start for iOS" screen. Choose Skip and Create App ID in the top right corner. Facebook will ask you to provide a display name for the app and a category. Enter what describes your business best and click "Create App ID" button. Figure 4-6 shows the screen after you click the button.

| iOS | Android | Facebook Canvas | Website |

Figure 4-6. Add a new iOS app with Facebook Developer Console

You might need to go through another security check screen before you can see the App ID, a 16-digit number. Write down this number; you will use it in our Xcode project.

You can add this key by editing the PLIST file of the Chapter 4 project source code, as shown in Figure 4-7.

1. Create a key called FacebookAppID with a string value, and add the 16-digit number app ID there.

2. Create a key called FacebookDisplayName with a string value, and add the Display Name we have had in the Facebook App Dashboard.

3. Create an array key called URL types with a single array subitem called URL Schemes. Give this a single item with your app ID prefixed with fb; it should look something like fb1235789899153886. Use the default parameter for Document Role: Editor.

Key	Type	Value
▼ Information Property List	Dictionary	(18 items)
FacebookDisplayName	String	Beauty & Me
FacebookAppID	String	1235789899153886
Localization native development r...	String	en
Executable file	String	$(EXECUTABLE_NAME)
Bundle identifier	String	com.ecommerceappbook.$(PRODUCT_NAME:rfc1034identifier)
InfoDictionary version	String	6.0
Bundle name	String	$(PRODUCT_NAME)
Bundle OS Type code	String	APPL
Bundle versions string, short	String	1.0
Bundle creator OS Type code	String	????
▼ URL types	Array	(1 item)
▼ Item 0 (Editor)	Dictionary	(2 items)
Document Role	String	Editor
▼ URL Schemes	Array	(1 item)
Item 0	String	fb1235789899153886

Chapter4 › Chapter4 › Supporting Files › Info.plist › No Selection

Chapter4
2 targets, iOS SDK 8.3
▼ Chapter4
  LoginSignup.Storyboard
  EMABDispatchViewController.m
  EMABDispatchViewController.h
  EMABAppDelegate.h
  EMABAppDelegate.m
  Main.storyboard
  Images.xcassets
  LaunchScreen.xib
▼ Supporting Files
  Info.plist
  main.m
  EMABConstants.h
  EMABConstants.m
  Product.h

Figure 4-7. Configure the Facebook Developer App ID with the Xcode project .plist file

Note   Facebook has detailed documentation about how to create a Facebook App. To learn more, go to `https://developers.facebook.com/docs/ios/getting-started`.

Manage Dependencies: Cocoapods

As an iOS developer, you should be familiar with Cocoapods. Cocoapods is the dependency manager for Swift and Objective-C Cocoa projects. It has thousands of libraries and can help you scale your projects elegantly.

If you have not installed Cocoapods on your Mac computer, this is the time to do so; you will use Cocopaods to install all Parse-related SDKs and other libraries.

> **Note** Visit `https://guides.cocoapods.org/using/getting-started.html#getting-started` to get started with Cocoapods and troubleshooting tips.

Install Cocoapods from the Terminal by running the following command:

```
$ sudo gem install cocoapods
```

Install the Podfile

Your Podfile consists of a few Parse-related libraries, the core Parse iOS SDK, the Parse UI iOS SDK, the Facebook iOS SDK, and ParseFacebookUtility iOS SDK. This is what your current Podfile looks like.

```
source 'https://github.com/CocoaPods/Specs.git'
pod 'Parse'
pod 'ParseFacebookUtils'
pod 'Facebook-iOS-SDK'
pod 'ParseUI'
```

This Podfile comes with Chapter 4 source code. After you have installed Cocoapods, simply run:

```
pod install
```

in your project directory. All dependent SDKs will be pulled and added to our project automatically. Remember, from now on, you will use Xcworkspace, which is created during the process of adding dependent SDKs.

When you want to keep up those dependent SDKs with the latest ones, you run the following command in a Terminal window whenever you set a fit:

```
pod update
```

Implement a Progress Indicator: SVProgressHud

In iOS development, it's common to show a pop-up message to tell a user some simple information such as content saved, error occurs, etc. The standard iOS way to handle this case is to use UIAlertController. For instance, to indicate to a user that a saving action is successful, use the following code:

```
UIAlertController* alert = [UIAlertController alertControllerWithTitle:@"Success"
                                                   message:@"Your data is saved."
                                         preferredStyle:UIAlertControllerStyleAlert];

    UIAlertAction* defaultAction = [UIAlertAction actionWithTitle:@"OK" style:UIAlertAction
    StyleDefault
                                   handler:^(UIAlertAction * action) {}];

    [alert addAction:defaultAction];
    [self presentViewController:alert animated:YES completion:nil];
```

The issue with UIAlertViewController is that a user has to tap the "OK" button to dismiss this alert. Implementation-wise, you have repeatedly written the same code over and over across an app.

To emphasize the implementation of the business logic of an e-commerce iPhone app, try to use dependent libraries as little as possible. However, I do want to introduce the SVProgessHud library. SVProgressHUD is a clean and easy-to-use HUD meant to display the progress of an ongoing task, or just simply display a message. To show a success message:

```
[SVProgressHUD showSuccessWithStatus:@"Successfully saved"];
```

To show an error message:

```
[SVProgressHUD showErrorWithStatus:[error localizedDescription]];
```

In either case, the SVProgressHud will be automatically dismissed after three seconds.

To show a data loading status and dismiss the status once the data loading is finished, you can use SVProgressHud in this way:

```
[SVProgressHUD show];
[product saveInBackgroundWithBlock:^(BOOL success, NSError *error) {
        [SVProgressHUD dismiss];
        if (!error) {
            [SVProgressHUD showSuccessWithStatus:@"Saved"];
        } else {
            [SVProgressHUD showErrorWithStatus:[error localizedDescription]];
        }
    }];
```

Now, you can edit your Podfile and add the SVProgressHud library dependency:

```
pod 'SVProgressHUD'
```

And update pods again:

```
pod update
```

> **Note**   To find more about SVProgressHud and how you can customize its appearance, go to
> https://github.com/TransitApp/SVProgressHUD.

Summary

In this chapter, I covered how to set up a Parse project on parse.com. I also introduced a custom class to keep track of important keys I obtained from Parse.com, Stripe.com, and Mailgun.com. I also gave a brief overview on how to apply for a Facebook Developer account and then set the Facebook App ID with the proposed app. In the last part of this chapter, I described the Podfile that you will use in this book.

Chapter 5

Product Category

The Beauty & Me sample app that accompanies this book presents products to users in a traditional way. First of all, we let users sell all brands we are carrying. If you don't know any brand, I will make up some, such as Origins, NUDE Skincare, etc. Under each brand, we have all products. When a user selects a product, the app displays the product detail. This chapter introduces the brand, or a more general name, product category.

In iOS app development, Model-View-Controller (MVC) is a widely used design pattern. I have structured the remaining chapters such that they follow this MVC pattern: first, I present the models used for implementing the feature discussed, then the views, and finally the controllers when applicable.

In this chapter, you learn about:

- The product category model
- The category view (UITableViewCell)
- The category controller
- Putting model, view, and controller together with UIStoryboard
- Adding sample data in Parse.com

Product Category Model

The Product Category model is used to mimic the makeup product brand. A brand has a title as the minimum, a logo, origin country, and a description about this brand. For this example, since I only carry well-known brands, I only use the brand title and logo image.

I have introduced PFObject in Chapter 3. Your category model will be a subclass of PFObject. Subclassing PFObject requires giving a ParseClassName. This ParseClassName needs to be the same you chose when setting it on the Parse website. In other words, if you create a model class called Category in your project on Parse.com, you need to use "Category" as the ParseClassName in the subclass file. The following sample code shows how this is done.

Start by registering a kCategory string constant with EMCAConstants.h:

```
extern NSString *const kCategory;
```

and in the EMABConstants.m file:

```
NSString *const kCategory = @"Category";
```

Next, create an EMABCategory subclass to represent your makeup product category. The class has two properties, title and image, which represent the brand name and logo. In Chapter 3, I explained how to create a PFObject subclass—for example, you use an NSString instance to hold the brand title and UIImage for the logo. The image file for each brand is stored on the Parse server; your iOS app will fetch the image file and convert it into UIImage, and then show the image with an UIImageView. Loading an image file from a remote server is always a challenging task in iOS. If you want to cache the image file so you don't need to fetch it again next time, you have more work to do.

Since this is a common task you are facing while developing an iOS app, Parse makes it easier by introducing a class called PFFile. I will use an example shortly to demonstrate how using this class makes a developers' live easier. For now, just use PFFile class to hold the image.

The iPhone app will also fetch all product categories from the Parse server. Chapter 3 introduced the PFQuery class. For this example, you will need to create a helper class method called +(PFQuery *)basicQuery in your EMABCategory subclass.

Here is the complete EMABCategory header file:

EMABCategory.h

```
#import <Parse/Parse.h>
@interface EMABCategory : PFObject<PFSubclassing>
@property (nonatomic, copy) NSString *title;
@property (nonatomic, strong) PFFile *image;
+(PFQuery *)basicQuery;
@end
```

If PFObject is not recognized, verify that you have included #import <Parse/Parse.h>.

The implementation of EMABCatgory is perhaps the simplest one in this book. Besides importing a header file of this subclass, you import "EMABConstants.h" because the required +(NSString *)ParseClassName method needs to return an NSString. You can write something like this:

```
+(NSString *)parseClassName {
    return @"Category";
}
```

If you use the @"Category" model class name at different locations but later on you want to change it to @"Brand," you have to look for it in the whole project and replace it with "Brand." Using a global constant helps to solve this issue. You just need to change it from "Category" to "Brand' in the "EMABConstants.m" once.

In the +(PFQuery *)basicQuery implementation, you sort the fetch results based on the title alphabetically by simply using "orderByAscending" method—this is another benefit of Parse. Imagine you develop for iOS, Android, or the Web. If you want to have the same features for the three platforms, platform engineers needs to write their own sorting method, given the back end doesn't have it, which is quite typical.

Here is the complete implementation:

EMABCategory.m

```
#import "EMABCategory.h"
#import  <Parse/PFObject+Subclass.h>
#import   "EMABConstants.h"

@implementation EMABCategory
@dynamic title, image;

+(NSString *)parseClassName
{
    return kCategory;
}

+(PFQuery *)basicQuery{
    PFQuery *query = [PFQuery queryWithClassName:[self parseClassName]];
    [query orderByAscending:@"title"];
    return query;

}
@end
```

Product Category View

As shown in the prototype of the sample app in Chapter 2, a UITableViewController is used to present all brands. While the UITableView itself looks pretty simple, what makes it look richer is each UITableViewCell, as shown in Figure 5-1. For the brand, focus on the UITableViewCell.

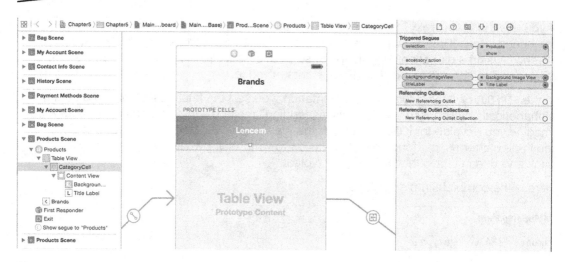

Figure 5-1. *Category cell in EMABCategoryTableViewController*

The EMABCategory has two properties, title and image; the EMABCategoryTableViewCell, a subclass of PFTableViewCell, also has two properties to hold the title and image: one is UILabel, the other is PFImageView.

You also want to let an EMABCategory model object hook up with EMABCategoryTableViewCell, so you create a helper method: -(void)configureItem:(EMABCategory *)item. Here is the complete header file:

EMABCategoryTableViewCell.h

```
#import "PFTableViewCell.h"
@class EMABCategory;
@interface EMABCategoryTableViewCell : PFTableViewCell
-(void)configureItem:(EMABCategory *)item;
@end
```

As you can see, you don't define the UILabel and PFImageView properties in the header file—you define them in the implementation file. The reason is that the properties are private; there is no need to let the outside world know what you are using. On the other hand, your UI is fairly simple, so for the purpose of keeping the code clean, you will use IBOutlet to hook up the properties in your implementation with the Main UIStoryboard. Here is the interface category in the .m file:

```
@interface EMABCategoryTableViewCell()
@property (nonatomic, weak) IBOutlet PFImageView *backgroundImageView;
@property (nonatomic, weak) IBOutlet UILabel *titleLabel;
@end;
```

The `titleLabel` will display a brand's title. Simple enough, use `self.titleLabel.text = item.title`. To display a brand's image, you use PFImageView and PFFile:

```
self.backgroundImageView.file = item.image;
[self.backgroundImageView loadInBackground];
```

The magic is `[self.backgroundImageView loadInBackground]`. It automatically handles async image loading and displaying, as well as caching.

Here is the complete implementation:

EMABCategoryTableViewCell.m

```objc
#import "EMABCategoryTableViewCell.h"
#import <ParseUI/PFImageView.h>
#import "EMABCategory.h"

@implementation EMABCategoryTableViewCell

-(void)configureItem:(EMABCategory *)item
{
    self.titleLabel.text = item.title;
    self.backgroundImageView.image = nil;
    if (item.image) {
        self.backgroundImageView.file = item.image;
        [self.backgroundImageView loadInBackground];
    } else {
        self.backgroundImageView.image = [UIImage imageNamed:@"category_cell_default_
        background"];
    }

}
@end
```

You may be wondering why I set `self.backgroundImageView.image = nil`. While UITableView reuses its UITableViewCell, the images in the old and offscreen cells will show before new images are loaded to replace those images. When you scroll UITableView, you will see the funky image refresh. There are a few different ways to solve this problem; one is in `-(void)prepareForReuse` in the UITableViewCell where you do it in `-(void)configureItem:(EMABCategory)item` for simplicity.

Product Category Controller

Next, you will be working on the controller.

First, create a new class named "EMABCategoriesTableViewController" and make sure it is a subclass of PFQueryTableViewController. I have already introduced PFQueryTableViewController in Chapter 3. In this view controller, you create a one-to-one mapping between the EMABCategory class and the EMABCateogryUITableViewCell. You will also use the features such as pull-to-refresh, pagination, and showing and dismissing a loading activity indicator before and after any data is loaded.

Here is the automatically generated header file:

EMABCategoriesTableViewController.h

```
#import <UIKit/UIKit.h>
#import <ParseUI/PFQueryTableViewController.h>
@interface EMABCategoriesTableViewController : PFQueryTableViewController

@end
```

In the .m implementation file, start by importing the necessary helper files such as "EMABConstants.h," "EMABCategory.h," and "EMABCategoryTableViewCell.h."

Next, implement the `-(void)awakeFromNib` method. `parseClassName`, `objectsPerPage`, and `pullToRefreshEnabled` are the properties of PFQueryTableViewController so you can just use them and set the values you want. In this case, the ParseClassName is defined by kCategory. You want to show 10 objects per page and enable pull-to-refresh. The activity loading indicator will be shown by default.

```
- (void)awakeFromNib {
    [super awakeFromNib];
    self.parseClassName = kCategory;
    self.paginationEnabled = YES;
    self.objectsPerPage = 10;
    self.pullToRefreshEnabled = YES;
}
```

Keep in mind you are using Storyboard to initialize your view controller so `-(void)awaeFromNib` method is a good place to enable pull-to-fresh, pagination, etc. If you use a different way such as `-(instancetype)initWithStyle:(UITableViewStyle)style`, then this method is the place for you to set ParseClassName, pagination, etc.

Next, you need to let the PFQueryTableViewController subclass know what kind of query you need to perform. You implement the method `-(PFQuery *)queryForTable`. In the EMABCategory class, you have defined a helper method called `+(PFQuery *)basicQuery`. Now you can just use it.

```
PFQuery *query = [EMABCategory basicQuery];
```

Or, you can just use the default implementation:

```
PFQuery *query = [PFQuery queryWithClassName:self.pasreClassName];
[query orderByAscending:@"title"];
```

If you end up using the same code a few more times, implementing it in the EMABCategory class makes more sense.

Next, PFQuery also has a method for you to manage cache policy: `kPFCachePolicyCacheThenNetwork`. This policy is quite self-explanatory. Keep in mind, when using `kPFCachePolicyCacheThenNetwork` as your caching policy your callback is always triggered twice. This is because the policy is to use the cache and then to go to the network, not to use the cache exclusively. There are other cache options such as kPFCachePolicyIgnoreCache, kPFCachePolicyCacheOnly, kPFCachePolicyNetworkOnly, kPFCachePolicyCacheElseNetwork, kPFCachePolicyNetworkElseCache, and kPFCachePolicyCacheThenNetwork.

```
if ([self.objects count] == 0) {
        query.cachePolicy = kPFCachePolicyCacheThenNetwork;
}
```

The complete implementation of +(PFQuery *)queryForTable looks like this:

```
-(PFQuery *)queryForTable {
    PFQuery *query = [EMABCategory basicQuery];
    if ([self.objects count] == 0) {
        query.cachePolicy = kPFCachePolicyCacheThenNetwork;
    }
    return query;
}
```

Next, implement the PFQueryTableViewController datasource method. First, you want to extent the default cell height, so you set the height of each cell to 60 points:

```
-(CGFloat)tableView:(UITableView *)tableView heightForRowAtIndexPath:(NSIndexPath *)
indexPath
{
    return 60.0;
}
```

PFQueryTableViewController has overridden the standard UITableView's -tableView:ce llForRowAtIndexPath: method. Namely, -tableView:cellForRowAtIndexPath:object:. Traditionally, you need the object array. Then you use indexPath.row to get the object for each row. Now you have this object automatically.

However, this override method assumes that you will give an object to each row and there is only one section. If you have multiple sections, this method won't work automatically.

Since you also enable pagination, and there are 10 objects on each page, each cell will be configured with an item. For this, you use the EMABCategoryTableViewCell -(void) configureItem:(EMABCategory *)item method.

You also need a way to load the next page. Here you add an extra cell after 10 objects. This cell has a title of "Load More...". If a user taps this cell, the app will load another 10 objects or one more page.

Here is the complete implementation:

```
- (EMABCategoryTableViewCell *)tableView:(UITableView *)tableView cellForRowAtIndexPath:
(NSIndexPath *)indexPath object:(EMABCategory *)object{
    EMABCategoryTableViewCell *cell = [tableView dequeueReusableCellWithIdentifier:
    @"CategoryCell" forIndexPath:indexPath];
    if (indexPath.row == [[self objects] count]) {
```

```
        cell.textLabel.text = NSLocalizedString(@"Load More…", @"");
    } else {
        [cell configureItem:object];
    }
    return cell;
}
```

The last step is to handle when a user taps "Load more…" and tap other CategoryCell. When the "Load more…" cell is tapped, another 10 objects are loaded and displayed in the table. Luckily, Parse has prepared this method for you. Simply call the method -(void) loadNextPage, and you are good to go.

A single tap on a brand cell displays all products under this brand (I will talk more about this in the next chapter).

Here is the complete implementation:

```
-(void)tableView:(UITableView *)tableView didSelectRowAtIndexPath:(NSIndexPath *)indexPath{
    if (indexPath.row == [[self objects] count]) {
        [self loadNextPage];
    } else {
        //todo
    }
}
```

Those are all the code parts. But there is still some more work you need to do in the UIStoryboard.

Putting It All Together: UIStoryboard

First, you need to set the brand UITableViewController introduced in Chapter 2 as your "EMABCategoryTableViewController." Figure 5-2 shows how to do this.

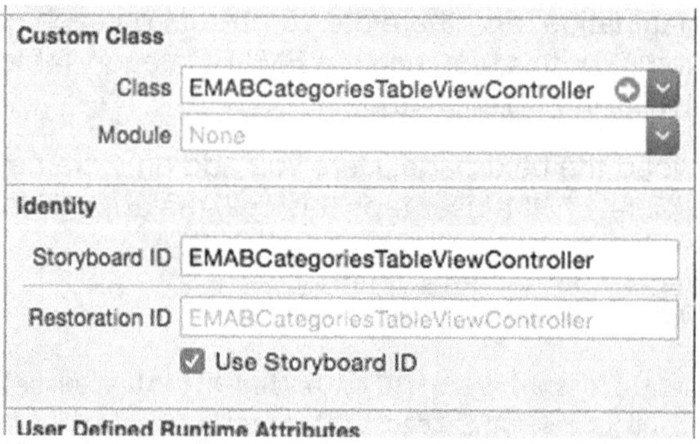

Figure 5-2. Set the Storyboard ID for a custom class

Personally, I also like to use the Class name as the Storyboard ID and Restoration ID to make sure they are unique.

Second, change TableView Content from Static Cells to Dynamic Protyotypes as shown in Figure 5-3.

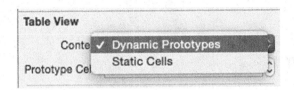

Figure 5-3. Use Dynamic Prototypes for the UITableViewCell

Then set the TableViewCell Style from "Basic" to "Custom," and an Identifier "CategoryCell" as shown in Figure 5-4.

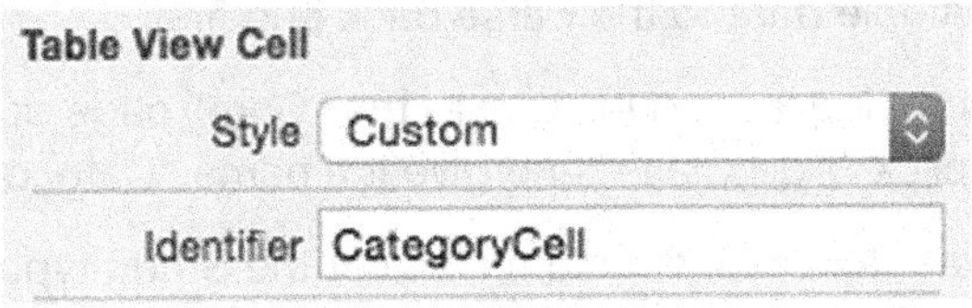

Table View Cell

Style	Custom
Identifier	CategoryCell

Figure 5-4. Use Custom Style

Also set the class of this cell "EMABCategoryTableViewCell," as shown in Figure 5-5.

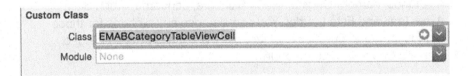

Figure 5-5. Use EMABCategoryTableViewCell class

Next, set the cell height to 60, as shown in Figure 5-6.

Table View Cell

Row Height   60 ☑ Custom

Figure 5-6. Set the Row Height

Finally, set the UIImageView to PFImageView, as shown in Figure 5-7.

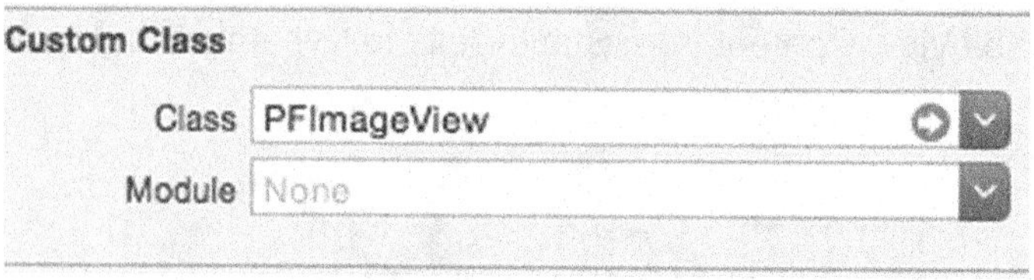

Custom Class

Class | PFImageView
Module | None

Figure 5-7. Use PFImageView

Now it's time to build and run this project.

Add Sample Data

If you followed along so far, the project will run just fine; but there is nothing to show. You need to add some sample data to the Parse back end first.

1. Go to Parse.com, log in, and browse to the "Core" page of the project. Then click "Add Class" and give it a name "Category."

2. Click "+Col" and, for the first column, select the String type and set its value to "title," then click "Create Column."

3. Click "+Col" again, this time select File type and set its value to image, then click "Create Column."

4. Next, add some sample data. For this sample, I have prepared seven (7) brands, namely, Original, Nade Skincare, Lencome, Fresh Skin, Aven, Diar, and Esta Louder. You can also use any pictures for those brands for demo purposes. Or just use the images I have included with the Chapter 5 source code.

5. Click the "+Row" button. Parse creates an empty row with "undefined" placeholder for each column. For this example, you only need to care about the "image" and "title" columns. Tap the "(undefined)" area in "Image" column. Parse asks you to upload an image. Upload an image. And set a title such as "Origins." When you press "Enter," Parse will automatically generate an objectId, createdAt, updatedAt and ACL for you. (I will cover ACL in Chapter 18.)

6. Repeat steps 5 six times to add six more rows.

Now when you return to your Xcode project or open the app in the simulator or your device, you should see the seven brands you just added when you build and run your project.

Summary

In this chapter, I covered how to implement the product brands feature. I introduced the EMABCategory model, EMABCategoryTableViewCell view, and the EMABCategoriesTableViewController controller. I also demonstrated how to connect the view, view controller with UIStoryboard. Finally, I talked about how to add sample data into Parse so your app can load data dynamically.

Chapter 6

The Products Screen

In this chapter, you will learn how to implement the Products screen. More specifically, you will learn how to display products and let users search your product list and filter products based on certain criteria. The first thing, however, is to create a product model.

The Product Model

Following the pattern introduced in earlier chapters, specify the model name in the EMABConstants helper class:

```
NSString *const kProduct= @"Product";
```

Next, create a new PFObject subclass, and name it "EMABProduct." If you look at a typical makeup product, you might need a lot of properties to describe a product. For example, EMABProduct model has the following properties: name, unit price, price unit, detail, thumbnail image, and full-size image. You also have to build a one-to-many relationship between product category and products so another important property is brand.

For this tutorial, use the following properties: name, detail (don't use description), price, priceUnit, thumbnail (for performance reason), and fullsizeImage; we have a pointer "brand" to EMABCategory. You will build a one-to-many relationship between EMABCategory and EMABProduct. One brand can have many products under this brand. Parse provides a few options and you can just directly use a pointer.

EMABProduct.h

```
#import <Parse/Parse.h>
@class EMABCategory;
@interface EMABProduct : PFObject<PFSubclassing>
@property (nonatomic, copy) NSString *name;
@property (nonatomic, copy) NSString *detail;
@property (nonatomic, assign) float unitPrice;
@property (nonatomic, copy) NSString *priceUnit;
```

```
@property (nonatomic, strong) PFFile *thumbnail;
@property (nonatomic, strong) PFFile *fullsizeImage;
@property (nonatomic, strong) EMABCategory *brand;
```

The last thing you need to do is to define a custom static method to query all products under one brand:

```
+(PFQuery *)queryForCategory:(EMABCategory *)brand;
```

When the properties of the priceUnit and the unitPrice are already defined (as I have done here), it's common to display a product price (e.g., $3.50/ea). You have to keep using the following format method when presenting the price on a UILabel:

```
[NSString stringWithFormat:@%@/%.2f, product.unitPrice, product.priceUnit];
```

To make things easier for yourself, create a helper method:

```
-(NSString *)friendlyPrice;
```

This suffices for now. You can add more helper methods or properties later if necessary. Next, continue with the implementation of the EMABProduct class.

Besides importing the necessary header files and the dynamic properties declaration, the +(NSString *)parseClassName will be:

```
+(NSString *)parseClassName
{
    return kProduct;
}
```

The +(PFQuery *)basicQuery method looks like this; here you will also sort all products by product name, as you have done with the brand.

```
+(PFQuery *)basicQuery {
    PFQuery *query = [PFQuery queryWithClassName:[self parseClassName]];
    [query orderByAscending:@"name"];
    return query;
}
```

If you want to sort products based on when each one is added to the Parse data store, you can use the following:

```
[query orderByDescending:@"createdAt"];
```

Your next query helper method is to query all products under one brand. The implementation might look like this:

```
+(PFQuery *)queryForCategory:(EMABCategory *)brand{
    PFQuery  *query = [self basicQuery];
    [query whereKey:@"brand" equalTo:brand];
    return query;
}
```

In this query method, the input parameter is an EMABCategory object. Make sure the brand property in EMABProduct is equal to this object.

```
[query whereKey:@"brand" equalTo:brand];
```

On the other hand, the +(PFQuery *)basicQuery method defines how you want to sort query results. It helps you create all kinds of query helper methods without having to repeat writing the same code over and over again.

The last method is -(NSString *)friendlyPrice:

```
-(NSString *)friendlyPrice{
    return [NSString localizedStringWithFormat:@"$ %.2f/%@", self.unitPrice, self.priceUnit];
}
```

The Product View

You will use a UITableView to display the product list. The key view for a UITableView is its cell. In Xcode, create a PFTableViewCell subclass and name it "EMABProductTableViewCell."

In the header file, add a helper method:

```
-(void)configureItem:(EMABProduct *)product;
```

to connect the EMABProduct model and this view. Here is the complete header file:

EMABProductTableViewCell

```
#import "PFTableViewCell.h"
@class EMABProduct;
@interface EMABProductTableViewCell : PFTableViewCell

-(void)configureItem:(EMABProduct *)product;

@end
```

Figure 6-1 shows what the product cell looks like.

Double Stay-in-Place Makeup

$ 37.00/ea

Figure 6-1. The Product TableView cell

This product cell consists of three UI elements: a UILabel to show the product name, a UILabel to show the product price, and a PFImage to show the product thumbnail.

Again, use EMABProductTableViewCell category to declare the properties:

```
@interface EMABProductTableViewCell()
@property (nonatomic, weak) IBOutlet UILabel *nameLabel;
@property (nonatomic, weak) IBOutlet UILabel *priceLabel;
@property (nonatomic, weak) IBOutlet PFImageView *thumbnailImageView;
@end
```

In the EMABProductTableViewCell cell, there is only one method -(void) configureItem:(EMABProduct*) product you need to implement.

At this point, your EMABProduct has the properties of name, unitPrice, priceUnit, and thumbnail; all you need to do is to assign the value of a product object to the EMABProductTableViewCell UI properties. EMABProduct has a helper method to generate a price with unit; you can use it as the text of priceLabel. To display the product's thumbnail, use the file of thumbnailImageView, and call the loadInBackground. The following code shows the complete implementation.

As discussed in Chapter 5, be sure to set thumbnailImageView to nil before you set its file to be the product's thumbnail. This ensures that ImageView will not show the old image before it displays the new image due to the UITableViewCell reuse nature. This is not the only way you can achieve this goal. For example, use -(void)prepareForUse method in UITableViewCell to handle this case.

```
-(void)prepareForReuse{
[super prepareForReuse];
self.nameLabel.text = @"";
self.priceLabel.text = @"";
self.thumbnailImageView.image = nil;
}

-(void)configureItem:(EMABProduct *)product{
    self.nameLabel.text = product.name;
    self.priceLabel.text = [product friendlyPrice];
    self.thumbnailImageView.image = nil;
    if (product.thumbnail) {
        self.thumbnailImageView.file = product.thumbnail;
        [self.thumbnailImageView loadInBackground];
    } else
        self.thumbnailImageView.image = [UIImage imageNamed:@"default_product_thumbnail"];

}
```

If there is no thumbnail file in the EMABProduct object, use a default image that comes with the project.

The Product Controller

You finished the view part. Now you can move to building the controller. In Xcode, create a new PFQueryTableViewController subclass EMABProductsTableViewController.

In the generated header file, declare a EMABCategory property. When a user selects a brand, show the product's view controller. In this view controller, you create a product query based on a brand. Use this brand property to connect a brand table view controller and products table view controller.

```
@property (nonatomic, strong) EMABCategory *brand;
```

Here is the complete EMABProductsTableViewController header file:

EMABProductsTableViewController.h

```
#import <UIKit/UIKit.h>
#import <ParseUI/PFQueryTableViewController.h>
@class EMABCategory;
@interface EMABProductsTableViewController : PFQueryTableViewController
@property (nonatomic, strong) EMABCategory *brand;
@end
```

In the implementation file, you need to have a brand setter method:

```
-(void)setBrand:(EMABCategory *)brand
{
    if (_brand != brand) {
        _brand = brand;
    }
}
```

The -(void)awakeFromNib method will look like this:

```
- (void)awakeFromNib {
    [super awakeFromNib];
    self.parseClassName = kProduct;
    self.objectsPerPage = 20;
    self.paginationEnabled = YES;
    self.pullToRefreshEnabled = YES;
}
```

Also, the -(PFQuery *)queryForTable method needs to take brand property into account:

```
- (PFQuery *)queryForTable {
    PFQuery *query = [EMABProduct queryForCategory:self.brand];
    if ([self.objects count] == 0) {
        query.cachePolicy = kPFCachePolicyCacheThenNetwork;
    }
    return query;
}
```

Next, customize the UITableView Datasource; in this case, set the cell height to 80.0 point:

```
-(CGFloat)tableView:(UITableView *)tableView heightForRowAtIndexPath:(NSIndexPath *)
indexPath
{
    return 80.0;
}
```

In the same way, use the PFQueryTableViewController custom method -tableView:cell ForRowAtIndexPath: to customize each cell based on given EMABProduct object. Since we load 20 objects each page, we add "Load more…" text on cell 21. The following code shows a complete implementation of the method. This method will return an instance of EMABProductTableViewCell. You also use the -(void)configureItem:(EMABProduct *)object method to connect a product object and its view.

```
- (EMABProductTableViewCell *)tableView:(UITableView *)tableView cellForRowAtIndexPath:
(NSIndexPath *)indexPath object:(EMABProduct *)object{
    EMABProductTableViewCell *cell = [tableView dequeueReusableCellWithIdentifier:@"ProductC
    ell" forIndexPath:indexPath];
    if (indexPath.row == [[self objects] count]) {
        cell.textLabel.text = NSLocalizedString(@"Load More…", @"");
    } else {
        [cell configureItem:object];
    }
    return cell;
}
```

The last method handles what happens when a user taps one of the cells. When the user taps a project cell, the app is supposed to display a product detail page. Since I have not discussed the product detail page yet, insert a comment (//todo) placeholder for now. When a user taps the "Load more…" cell, the next 20 products are loaded. Here is the complete implementation:

```
-(void)tableView:(UITableView *)tableView didSelectRowAtIndexPath:(NSIndexPath *)indexPath{
    if (indexPath.row == [[self objects] count]) {
        [self loadNextPage];
    } else {
        //todo
    }
}
@end
```

You are almost ready to run the app in a simulator or on your device. Only one more implementation in EMABCategoriesTableViewController is missing. After a user taps a brand cell, the Products table view controller should be loaded. Go to EMABCategoriesTableViewC ontroller.m and add the following code:

```
-(void)tableView:(UITableView *)tableView didSelectRowAtIndexPath:(NSIndexPath *)indexPath{
    if (indexPath.row == [[self objects] count]) {
        [self loadNextPage];
```

```
    } else {
            EMABProductsTableViewController *viewController = [self.storyboard
            instantiateViewControllerWithIdentifier:@"EMABProductsTableViewController"];
NSIndexPath *indexPath = [self.tableView indexPathForSelectedRow];
            [viewController setBrand:self.objects[indexPath.row]];
[self.navigationController pushViewController:viewController];
    }
}
```

Now you can build and run your project, to make sure there is no error.

Add Sample Data

So far, you have not added any product for any brand yet, so there is nothing to show after you tap a brand. You need to add some product data to the Parse back end.

Go to Parse.com, log in, and browse to "Core" page of the sample project. Then click "Add Class" and give it a name "Product."

Next, click "+Col"; for the first col, select the String type and set its value to "name," then click "Create Column." In the same way, add "detail" column with String type, "unitPrice" with Number type, "priceUnit" with String type, "thumbnail" with PFFile type, and "fullsizeImage" with PFFile type. The last one is important; we add a column with a "brand" column with Pointer Type, which should point to "Category" class. See Figure 6-2 to see the details.

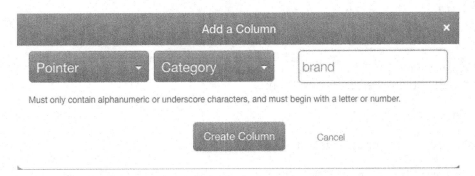

Figure 6-2. Add a Pointer type in Parse

Now it's time to add product data. I have prepared three Esta Louder products. You can also find images for these brands for demo purposes. Or just use the images I have prepared for the Chapter 6 project source code.

Next, click the "+Row" button. Parse creates an empty row with an "undefined" placeholder for each column. You have multiple columns to fill. One of the most important ones is the "brand" column.

First, tap "Category" class and find the row for Esta Louder. Copy the value of the "objectId" column for this row. Then move to "Product" class, tap the "(undefined)" area in "brand" column, and paste the "objectId" value. Now you can add a product name, product summary, unit price, and use "ea" for priceUnit; then upload a thumbnail and full-size image for this product.

Following the previous steps, add two more rows.

Return to your Xcode project or open the app on the simulator or your device. Now, on the brand screen, when you tap the Esta Louder cell, you should see the three products you just added.

Add a Search Feature

One of the required features for the app is that a customer can search products based on part of a product name in the product list view. When dealing with searching, one can implement to only search from loaded data, or search your back-end data store to find all matches. Obviously searching from loaded data is much quicker, but the results are also limited. It might turn out results are not found. So the best approach is to search on the back end.

Currently search in the app is limited. A user can only search products based on product names. For example, an Esta Louder product name contains the "Night Repair" string. If a user enters "Night" in a search box, the app won't find all products whose name or detail contains "Night." And the search keyword is case sensitive. If a user enters "night" instead of "Night," all products whose names contain "Night" won't be returned. To get around this limitation, you can preprocess the user's input and capitalize each word.

First, add a new query method to the EMABProduct model class. Declare this method in the header file:

EMABProduct.h

```
+(PFQuery *)queryForCategory:(EMABCategory *)brand keyword:(NSString *)keyword;
```

In its implementation, call the +(PFQuery *)queryForCategory:(EMABCategory *)brand method, and add another query condition:

```
- whereKey:containsString:
```

Here is the complete implementation:

```
+(PFQuery *)queryForCategory:(EMABCategory *)brand keyword:(NSString *)keyword
{
    PFQuery *query = [self queryForCategory:brand];
    [query whereKey:@"name" containsString:keyword];
    return query;
}
```

Next, to the controller. There are a few places you need to implement.

First, you need to keep track of the user's search keyword; add a new property in the EMABProductsTableViewController category:

```
@property (nonatomic, copy) NSString *keyword;
```

Second, you also need to declare UISearchBar delegate protocol in the class category:

```
@interface EMABProductsTableViewController()<UISearchBarDelegate>
```

Third, you need to connect the UISearchbar to view controller delegate (you already added a UISearchBar in controller xib file in Chapter 5). Figure 6-3 shows how to connect it.

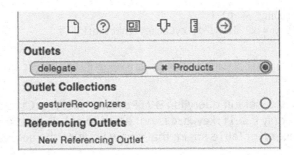

Figure 6-3. *The UISearchBar delegate*

Here is the complete implementation:

EMABProductsTableViewController.m

```
@interface EMABProductsTableViewController()<UISearchBarDelegate>
@property (nonatomic, weak) IBOutlet UISearchBar *searchBar;
@property (nonatomic, copy) NSString *keyword;
@end;
```

Fourth, implement the UISearchBar delegate method:

```
- (void)searchBarSearchButtonClicked:(UISearchBar *)searchBar
{
    if ([searchBar.text length] > 0) {
        [searchBar resignFirstResponder];
        self.keyword = searchBar.text;
        [self clear];
        [self loadObjects];
    }
}
```

Check if there is any text in the search bar (searchBar). If there is, dismiss the keyboard, let the keyword be the searchBar's text, and call the PFQueryTableViewController's method, -(void)clear, to clear the UITableView. Finally, use another PFQueryTableViewController's method -(void)loadObjects to fire up another query. This time, use a different query for this search purpose.

Fifth, modify - (PFQuery *)queryForTable as shown here:

```
- (PFQuery *)queryForTable {
    PFQuery *query = [EMABProduct queryForCategory:self.brand];

    if (self.keyword) {
        query = [EMABProduct queryForCategory:self.brand keyword:self.keyword];
    }
    if ([self.objects count] == 0) {
        query.cachePolicy = kPFCachePolicyCacheThenNetwork;
    }
    return query;
}
```

In this implementation, the default query is [EMABProduct queryForCategory:self.brand]. A search query is done only if self.keyword is not equal to nil. In step 4, [self loadObjects] will use -(PFQuery *)queryForTable again; that's how you use the queryForCategory: keyword:

```
if (self.keyword) {
        query = [EMABProduct queryForCategory:self.brand keyword:self.keyword];
}
```

For this reason, you need to set self.keyword to nil after we finish the search. You can do it at -(void)viewWillAppear

```
-(void)viewWillAppear:(BOOL)animated
{
    [super viewWillAppear:animated];
    self.keyword = nil;
}
```

Sometimes a user intents to perform a search, taps the UISearchBar, but then decides to give up. Tapping UISearchBar will bring up the soft keyboard; so you need to dismiss the keyboard.

Add a Filter Option

As part of the product feature, a user can filter products based on properties such as price. Similarly, you can filter products from loaded results, or query the remote server to get new results based on query criteria. In this implementation, you learn how to query your remote server.

In the sample app's UI design, when a user taps a "Filter" bar button item, and a new UIViewController will be shown. The user will slide two sliders to determine the minimum and maximum price he or she is interested in. Once the price range is set, the user taps the "Done" bar button item. This view controller will be dismissed and the product list view controller will be updated with new search results. Figure 6-4 shows all UI elements.

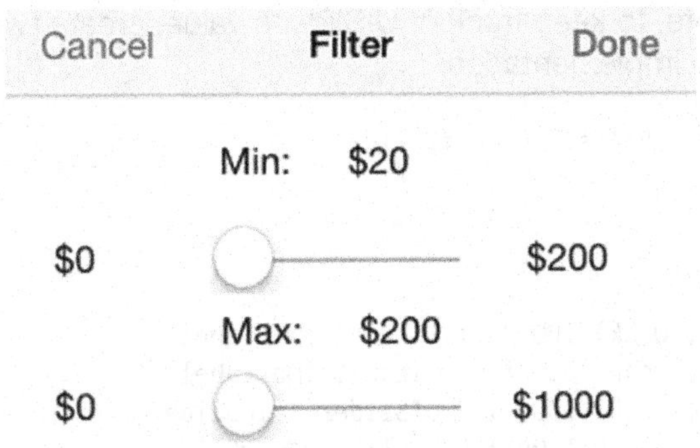

Cancel   **Filter**   Done

Min: $20

$0   ◯———— $200

Max: $200

$0   ◯———— $1000

Figure 6-4. The EMABProductsFilterViewController UI elements

First, add a new method in the EMABProduct model class. In the header file, declare this method as shown here:

EMABProduct.h

```
+(PFQuery *)queryForCategory:(EMABCategory *)brand minPrice:(float)min maxPrice:(float)max;
```

In this method, you query a brand based on the minimum price and the maximum price a user specifies.

For the implementation, use PFQuery's -whereKey:lessThanOrEqualTo: and -whereKey:greaterThanOrEqualTo: to help filter products from server.

EMABProduct.m

```
+(PFQuery *)queryForCategory:(EMABCategory *)brand minPrice:(float)min maxPrice:(float)max{
    PFQuery *query = [self queryForCategory:brand];
    [query whereKey:@"price" greaterThanOrEqualTo:@(min)];
    [query whereKey:@"price" lessThanOrEqualTo:@(max)];
    return query;
}
```

Next, create a new UIViewController subclass "EMABProductsFilterViewController." In its header file, create one typedef to make the code a bit more readable:

```
typedef void (^ViewControllerDidFinish)(EMABProductsFilterViewController *viewController,
float minPrice, float maxPrice);
```

The one is used to handle after a user taps the "Done" bar button item.

Continue to create two interface properties:

```
@property (nonatomic, copy) ViewControllerDidFinish finishBlock;
```

There are quite a few things you need to do just to handle the set of price ranges. First, use two ivars to keep track of the minimum and the maximum price. Since you also need to update your view controller UI of what the current slider value is, you also need another

UILabels. Furthermore, to keep track of UISlider's value, create two properties for them. Here is the complete implementation:

```
@interface EMABProductsFilterViewController (){
    float minPrice;
    float maxPrice;
}

@property (nonatomic, weak) IBOutlet UILabel *minLabel;
@property (nonatomic, weak) IBOutlet UILabel *maxLabel;
@property (nonatomic, weak) IBOutlet UISlider *minSlider;
@property (nonatomic, weak) IBOutlet UISlider *maxSlider;

@end
```

In the implementation, initialize your ivars in -(void)viewDidLoad:

```
- (void)viewDidLoad {
    [super viewDidLoad];

    minPrice = 0.0;
    maxPrice = 0.0;
}
```

Create an IBAction method for two UISliders, call it onSlider. When a user slides any of the sliders, update its value to UILabel. Also let minPrice and maxPrice keep track of the sliders' value.

```
-(IBAction)onSlider:(id)sender{
    UISlider *slider = (UISlider *)sender;
    NSString *friendlySliderValue = [NSString stringWithFormat:@"%.0f",slider.value];;
    if (slider.tag == 99) {
        minPrice = slider.value;
        self.minLabel.text = friendlySliderValue;
    } else {
        maxPrice = slider.value;
        self.maxLabel.text = friendlySliderValue;
    }
}
```

Add an IBAction for the "Cancel" bar button item as shown in the following snippet; basically, you just pop the current view controller:

```
-(IBAction)onCancel:(id)sender{

    [self.navigationController popViewControllerAnimated:YES];
}
```

Finally, add an IBAction for the "Done" bar button item as shown in the following snippet. How do you handle the case when a user has not done anything but just tap "Done"? In this scenario, you will remind the user that you need more information or the user needs to enter his or her input more accurately.

```
-(IBAction)onDone:(id)sender{
    if (minPrice > 0 && minPrice < maxPrice) {
        UIAlertView *alertView = [[UIAlertView alloc] initWithTitle:NSLocalizedString
        (@"Error", @"Error") message:NSLocalizedString(@"Please make sure your max price is
        greater than your min price.", @"") delegate:nil cancelButtonTitle:NSLocalizedString
        (@"OK", @"OK") otherButtonTitles:nil, nil];
        [alertView show];
    } else {
        self.finishBlock(self, minPrice, maxPrice);
        [self.navigationController popViewControllerAnimated:YES];
    }
}

@end
```

Finally, return back to EMABProductsViewController. In a similar fashion, add two ivars:

```
@interface EMABProductsTableViewController()<UISearchBarDelegate>{
    float minPrice;
    float maxPrice;
}
```

Next, add the following IBAction method to handle while a user taps "Filter" bar button item. In this method, you will need to do a few things. First, present the EMABProductsFilterViewController; then, handle the minimum and maximum price a user sets; next, clear the current table view; and finally, perform a query. Here is the complete implementation.

```
-(IBAction)onFilter:(id)sender
{
    EMABProductsFilterViewController *viewController =
    (EMABProductsFilterViewController *)[self.storyboard
    instantiateViewControllerWithIdentifier:@"EMABProductsFilterViewController"];

  viewController.finishBlock = ^(EMABProductsFilterViewController *viewControlle, float
  minValue, float maxValue){
        minPrice = minValue;
        maxPrice = maxValue;
        self.keyword = nil;
        [self clear];
        [self loadObjects];
    };

    [self.navigationController presentViewController:viewController animated:YES
    completion:nil];
}
```

Lastly, you need to modify -(PFQuery *)queryForTable as shown here:

```
- (PFQuery *)queryForTable {
    PFQuery *query = [EMABProduct queryForCategory:self.brand];

    if (self.keyword) {
        query = [EMABProduct queryForCategory:self.brand keyword:self.keyword];
    }

  if (minPrice > 0 && maxPrice>0) {
   query = [EMABProduct queryForCategory:self.brand minPrice:minPrice maxPrice:maxPrice];
}
    if ([self.objects count] == 0) {
        query.cachePolicy = kPFCachePolicyCacheThenNetwork;
    }
    return query;
}
```

Don't forget to connect "Filter" UIBarButtonItem to the method.

Now it's time to build and run the project.

Summary

In this chapter, I covered the topics of showing a product list under a product category, searching products based on name, and filtering products based on price.

7

The Product Detail Screen

In this chapter you learn how to implement the product detail screen, which includes information such as the product name, price, detail, and full-size image; the screen also includes a share menu as well as the option to buy a product or add it to a favorites list.

Build the Product Detail Screen

Figure 7-1 shows the finished UI of the product detail screen. The UI uses the UINavigationBar title to show the product's name; the right bar button item to add the share options; and a "heart" button so users can add the product to their Favorites list. To show the product's name and price, you use two UILabels. The product detail might be pretty lengthy, so you use a UITextView to hold its content. Finally, you use a plain button labeled "Add to Bag" to let a user add this product to the shopping bag.

Figure 7-1. *The finished product detail user interface*

Here's how you implement the UI. First, create a UIViewController subclass, EMABProductDetailViewController. In the generated header file, create a property:

```
@property (nonatomic, strong) EMABProduct *product;
```

Next, pass a selected EMABProduct instance from the previous product list to this product detail. The property you created serves this purpose. Here is the complete implementation:

EMABProductDetailViewController.h

```
#import <UIKit/UIKit.h>

@class EMABProduct;
@interface EMABProductDetailViewController : UIViewController

@property (nonatomic, strong) EMABProduct *product;

@end
```

In the implementation file, you need a PFImageView property to display the full-size image of the product, a UILabel to display the product's name, a UILabel to display its price, and a UITextView to show its detail. You also need a custom button that a user can tap to add the product to the Favorites list. Here is the full code:

```
@interface EMABProductDetailViewController ()
@property (nonatomic, weak) IBOutlet PFImageView *fullsizeImageView;
@property (nonatomic, weak) IBOutlet UILabel *productNameLabel;
```

```
@property (nonatomic, weak) IBOutlet UILabel *productPriceLabel;
@property (nonatomic, weak) IBOutlet UITextView *detailTextView;
@property (nonatomic, weak) IBOutlet UIButton *heartButton;
@end
```

In the implementation, first implement the EMABProduct property setter:

```
-(void)setProduct:(EMABProduct *)product{
    if (_product !=product) {
        _product = product;

        [self updateUI];
    }

}
```

In this setter, also use a helper method, -(void)updateUI. You might need to update the whole UI on multiple occasions (which is what I usually do). Instead of handling UI updates all over the place, I use one method that is called in the -(void)viewDidLoad method as shown here:

```
- (void)viewDidLoad {
    [super viewDidLoad];
    [self updateUI];
}
```

This updateUI method does one thing for right now: it connects the model and view. Here is the full code:

```
-(void)updateUI{
    if (self.product.fullsizeImage) {
        self.fullsizeImageView.file = self.product.fullsizeImage;
        [self.fullsizeImageView loadInBackground];
    }

    self.productNameLabel.text = self.product.name;
    self.productPriceLabel.text = [self.product friendlyPrice];
    self.detailTextView.text = [self.product detail];
}
```

Next, implement the IBAction that is triggered when a user taps the "Add to Bag" button. When the button is tapped, you need to check whether the customer is a valid, registered user or just a visitor. To do so, use the Parse [PFUser currentUser] method. In the case of registered user, [PFUser currentUser] will return an instance, otherwise it will return a nil. At this point, you want to ask users to sign up for an account or log in (if they haven't done so already). I will discuss how to handle the "Add to Bag" request in a later chapter. For now, here is how you alert the user to sign up or log in:

```
-(IBAction)onBag:(id)sender
{
    if (! [PFUser currentUser]) {
        [self showWarning];
    } else {
        //todo:
    }
}
```

In this sample code, the helper method `-(void)showWarning` reminds the user. You will use it again on another occasion, so it's best to create a common method:

```
-(void)showWarning
{
    [[[UIAlertView alloc] initWithTitle:NSLocalizedString(@"Warning", @"Warning")
    message:NSLocalizedString(@"Please sign up or log in", @"") delegate:nil
    cancelButtonTitle:NSLocalizedString(@"Later", @"Later") otherButtonTitles:
    NSLocalizedString(@"OK", @"OK"), nil] show];
}
```

This implementation only throws a warning. A better way is to bring up the signup or login screen when the user taps "OK."

Add Share Options

An important feature of the app is the Share option or menu. To add this feature, use UIActivityViewController. Using the UIActivityViewController is pretty straightforward to use (to learn more about it, refer to the iOS documentation). First, you create what you want to share, instantiate a UIActivityViewController instance, define what services are not used for this share purpose, and then present the instance. Figure 7-2 shows a UIActivityViewController from the user's point of view.

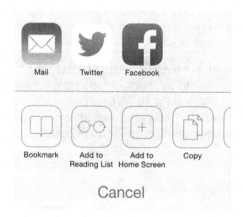

Figure 7-2. The UIActivityViewController from a user's point of view

Here is the full code:

```objc
-(IBAction)onShare:(id)sender {

    NSString *textToShare = [NSString stringWithFormat:@"%@, %@", self.product.name,
    [self.product friendlyPrice]];
    NSURL *imageUrl = [NSURL URLWithString:self.product.fullsizeImage.url];

    NSArray *objectsToShare = @[textToShare, imageUrl];

    UIActivityViewController *activityVC = [[UIActivityViewController alloc]
    initWithActivityItems:objectsToShare applicationActivities:nil];

    NSArray *excludeActivities = @[
    ........................UIActivityTypeAssignToContact,
                            UIActivityTypeSaveToCameraRoll,
                        UIActivityTypePostToFlickr,
                            UIActivityTypePostToVimeo];

    activityVC.excludedActivityTypes = excludeActivities;
    [self presentViewController:activityVC animated:YES completion:nil];
}
```

Keep in mind, this is a dramatically simplified API. All available services don't necessarily support the data content users may want to share. You may also want to add even more content for the services you want to support.

Add a Favorites List

To implement the Favorites list feature, you need a new model class.

In Xcode, create a new PFObject subclass and name it "EMABFavoriteProduct." This model has two properties—PFUser and EMABProduct—to represent that a user liked a product. In other words, this model class is a use case of the Parse joining tables relationship. Every time a user likes a product, a record is created in this model class. You might think this is redundant. You could use another approach; for instance, you could use a favorite array for this user. After all, there is one user but many favorite products, so using an array definitely works in this case. The advantage of using the joining tables method, however, is that the code is quite clean.

To get a user's Favorites list, use PFQuery. Create a basic PFQuery method and customize it to your needs. Here is the complete code:

EMABFavoriteProduct.h

```objc
#import <Parse/Parse.h>
@class EMABProduct;
@interface EMABFavoriteProduct : PFObject<PFSubclassing>
@property (nonatomic, strong) PFUser *customer;
@property (nonatomic, strong) EMABProduct *product;
```

```
+(PFQuery *)basicQuery;
+(PFQuery *)queryForCustomer:(PFUser *)customer;
+(PFQuery *)queryForCustomer:(PFUser *)customer product:(EMABProduct *)product;
@end
```

In this snippet you have two extra helper queries: +(PFQuery *)queryForCustomer:(PFUser *) customer gets a list of favorite products for a user; +(PFQuery *)queryForCustomer:(PFUser *) customer product:(EMABProduct *)product checks whether the user has a product in the Favorites list.

In to EMABConstants.h add a new NSString constant, kFavoriteProduct, and implement it in EMABConstants.m file.

```
NSString *const kFavoriteProduct = @"FavoriteProduct";
```

In the required +(NSString *)parseClassName method, use the NSString constant to represent the model's name.

```
+(NSString *)parseClassName
{
    return kFavoriteProduct;
}
```

In the +(PFQuery *)basicQuery method, sort the result based on when it is created. You can also use the PFQuery -include: method to include the user and product data. This is required to show either the product detail or the user's detail.

```
+(PFQuery *)basicQuery
{
    PFQuery *query = [PFQuery queryWithClassName:[self parseClassName]];
    [query orderByDescending:@"createdAt"];
    [query include:@"customer"];
    [query include:@"product"];
    return query;
}
```

In the +(PFQuery *)queryForCustomer:(PFUser *)customer method, use the PFQuery query condition method -whereKey: equalTo:

```
+(PFQuery *)queryForCustomer:(PFUser *)customer {
    PFQuery *query = [self basicQuery];
    [query whereKey:@"customer" equalTo:customer];
    return query;

}
```

Then implement +(PFQuery *)queryForCustomer:(PFUser *)customer product:
(EMABProduct *)product:

```
+(PFQuery *)queryForCustomer:(PFUser *)customer product:(EMABProduct *)product
{
    PFQuery *query = [self queryForCustomer:customer];
    [query whereKey:@"product" equalTo:product];
    return query;
}

@end
```

That's the EMABFavoriteProduct. Don't forget to register this PFSubclass at AppDelegate
by calling:

```
[EMABFavoriteProduct registerSublcass];
```

Next, go to the EMABProductDetailViewController.m file. In the -(void)viewDidLoad method,
check whether the user has already liked the product, given there is a valid user.

```
- (void)viewDidLoad {
    [super viewDidLoad];
    [self updateUI];
    [ self checkIfFavorited];
}
```

The checkIfFfavorited method verifies whether there is a record on the back-end server.
If true, the favorite button is disabled. You also want to check that the server is queried
only if there is a valid user.

```
-(void)checkIfFavorited
{
    if (! [PFUser currentUser]) {
        PFQuery *fPQuery = [EMABFavoriteProduct queryForCustomer:[PFUser currentUser]
        product:self.product];
        [fPQuery getFirstObjectInBackgroundWithBlock:^(PFObject *object, NSError *error){
            if (!error) {
                self.heartButton.enabled = false;
            }
        }];
    }
}
@end
```

You also want to allow users to add the product to their Favorites lists. The "heart" button is
connecting to an IBOutlet method -(IBAction)onFavorite:(id)sender.

Only a user who signed up or logged in can add products to the shopping bag, or like a product. So first you need to check whether there is a valid user. If so, create a new FavoriteProduct object, and save it to the Parse back end. Once saved successfully, alert the user with a success message. Here is a full code:

```
-(IBAction)onFavorite:(id)sender{
    if ( ![PFUser currentUser]) {
        [self showWarning];
    } else {
        EMABFavoriteProduct *favoriteProduct = [EMABFavoriteProduct object];
        [favoriteProduct setCustomer:[PFUser currentUser]];
        [favoriteProduct setProduct:self.product];
        [favoriteProduct saveInBackgroundWithBlock:^(BOOL success, NSError *error){
            if (!error) {
                [SVProgressHud showSuccessWithStatus: :NSLocalizedString(@"Successfully
                added", @""];
            }

        }];
    }
}
```

Summary

In this chapter, I covered the implementation of showing a product detail, sharing the product details to different services available on a user's phone, and adding a product to the user's Favorites list (provided that it has not been added to the list previously). The favorite product feature is implemented using a join table model class, EMABFavoriteProduct. I also emphasized the importance of the -include: method in PFQuery for fetching the user's data or the product's data when fetching the user's Favorites list.

Chapter 8

The Sign-Up Feature

In the previous chapter, you learned how to alert a user to sign up or log in when adding a product to the shopping bag or to the Favorites list. In this chapter, you implement a dispatch screen that enables users to create an account, log into an existing account, or log in with Facebook. You also learn how to sign up customers. How to implement the direct log in and log in with Facebook features are covered in Chapter 9.

Build a Dispatch Screen

When you implemented the main dispatch feature, you created a different UIStoryboard named LoginSignupStoryboard to reduce the workload of Main.storyboard.

The UI of this DispatchViewController is pretty simple. There are three buttons: the button labeled "Sign Up" is for showing the sign-up screen; the buttons labeled "Log In" and "Log In with Facebook" will be covered in Chapter 9.

To simplify the main view controller, use the segues in the LoginSignUpStoryboard to connect the "Sign Up" button to the EMABSignUpViewController, connect the "Log In" button to EMABLoginViewController, and set up an IBAction for "Log In with Facebook."

Also provide a "Cancel" UIBarButtonItem in case the user doesn't want to log in or sign up for an account at this point, so he or she can leave the screen. This LoginSignUpStoryboard is implemented with its own UINavigationController, so you can simply use:

```
[self dismissViewControllerAnimated:YES completion:nil];
```

to dismiss the dispatch screen.

Here is the full implementation:

```
@implementation EMABDispatchViewController

- (void)viewDidLoad {
    [super viewDidLoad];

}

-(IBAction)onFacebookLogin:(id)sender{
    //todo
}

-(IBAction)onCancel:(id)sender{
    [self dismissViewControllerAnimated:YES completion:nil];
}
@end
```

The Sign-up Model

Let's jump into the User model, EMABUser, a subclass of PFUser. By default, the EMABUser class has the properties username, password, and e-mail, which are inherited from PFUser; you also may want to collect a little bit more information from the user such as name, address, and photo. Here is the full implementation:

EMABUser.h

```
#import <Parse/Parse.h>
@interface EMABUser : PFUser<PFSubclassing>
@property (nonatomic, copy) NSString *firstName;
@property (nonatomic, copy) NSString *lastName;
@property (nonatomic, assign) int gender;
@property (nonatomic, copy) NSString *phone;
@property (nonatomic, copy) NSString *address1;
@property (nonatomic, copy) NSString *address2;
@property (nonatomic, copy) NSString *city;
@property (nonatomic, copy) NSString *state;
@property (nonatomic, copy) NSString *zipcode;
@property (nonatomic, copy) PFFile *photo;
+(EMABUser *)currentUser;
@end
```

When signing up a user, you only need the user to enter an e-mail address and password. When the user purchases something, you need to know where to ship your products to, so you need to ask the user to enter a shipping address until then. You also provide the Facebook login feature so you can get more information about the user such as a profile photo, gender, region, relationship, and interests. This requires different permissions from the user and Facebook. For now, only ask for the user's gender and photo.

You also want to override +(PFUser *)currentUser method to return an EMABUser, or Xcode will keep warning you about it.

Here is the EMABUser implementation part:

EMABUser.m

```
#import "EMABUser.h"
#import <Parse/PFObject+Subclass.h>
@implementation EMABUser
@dynamic firstName, lastName, gender, phone, address1, address2, city, state, zipcode,
photo;

+(EMABUser *)currentUser{
    return (EMABUser *)[PFUser currentUser];
}
@end
```

The Sign-up View

The Sign-Up screen consists of a UITableView, a button with a "Sign Up" title, and a Bar Button Item with the title of "Sign Up."

UITableView has three cells. For each cell, use a UITextField to capture a user's input. The first cell is for the registration e-mail, the second cell is for the registration password, and the third cell is for the password confirmation.

Since you will show a similar UITableView with UITextField UITableViewCell, create a UITextField subclass to eliminate redundancies.

First, create the EMABEmailTextField class.

EMABEmailTextField.h

```
#import <UIKit/UIKit.h>

@interface EMABEmailTextField : UITextField

@end
```

EMABEmailTextField.m

```
#import "EMABEmailTextField.h"

@implementation EMABEmailTextField

-(instancetype)initWithFrame:(CGRect)frame
{
    self = [super initWithFrame:frame];
    if (self) {
        self.borderStyle = UITextBorderStyleNone;
        self.textColor = [UIColor blackColor];
        self.autocapitalizationType = UITextAutocapitalizationTypeNone;
        self.placeholder = NSLocalizedString(@"Email", @"");
        self.backgroundColor = [UIColor whiteColor];
```

```
        self.autocorrectionType = UITextAutocorrectionTypeNo; . . . // no auto correction
        support

        self.keyboardType = UIKeyboardTypeEmailAddress; . . . // use the default type input
        method (entire keyboard)
        self.returnKeyType = UIReturnKeyDone;

        self.clearButtonMode = UITextFieldViewModeWhileEditing; . . . // has a clear 'x'
        button to the right

        // Add an accessibility label that describes what the text field is for.
        [self setAccessibilityLabel:NSLocalizedString(@"Email", @"")];

    }

    return self;
}
@end
```

In this implementation, you set the border style, text color, placeholder text, background color, keyboard type and auto correction type, and clear button mode to provide a better UI and user experience.

Next, create EMABPasswordTextField to customize the password TextField look and feel. Here is the implementation:

EMABPasswordTextField.h

```
#import <UIKit/UIKit.h>

@interface EMABPasswordTextField : UITextField

@end
```

EMABPasswordTextField.m

```
#import "EMABPasswordTextField.h"

@implementation EMABPasswordTextField

-(instancetype)initWithFrame:(CGRect)frame
{
    self = [super initWithFrame:frame];
    if (self) {
        self.borderStyle = UITextBorderStyleNone;
        self.textColor = [UIColor blackColor];
        self.placeholder = NSLocalizedString(@"Password",@"");
        self.backgroundColor = [UIColor whiteColor];

        self.keyboardType = UIKeyboardTypeDefault;
        self.returnKeyType = UIReturnKeyDone;
        self.secureTextEntry = YES;    // make the text entry secure (bullets)
```

```
        self.clearButtonMode = UITextFieldViewModeWhileEditing;
        // has a clear 'x' button to the right
        [self setAccessibilityLabel:NSLocalizedString(@"Password", @"")];
    }

    return self;

}

@end
```

This looks pretty similar to the EMABEmailTextField; the big difference is that you need to use the secureTextEntry property to hide a user's input.

Note that it's not necessary to use a UiTableView with UITextField in UITableViewCell—it just looks nicer. Some developers choose to put three UITextFields on top of a background image with a few separate lines. It also works nicely, if you can find this kind of background image.

The Sign-up Controller

Next, get ready for the EMABSignUpViewController implementation.

First, create the EMABSignUpViewController class as a subclass of UIViewController. There is not too much you need to do with its header file; focus on the implementation file instead. Since you have used UITableView, you need to put the protocol of UITableView in place. You also have UITextField in place, so it's a good idea to use the UITextField Delegate protocol; this lets you dismiss the keyboard when the user taps the "Done" button. Here is the implementation:

EMABSignupViewController.m

```
#import "EMABSignupViewController.h"
#import "EMABConstants.h"
#import "EMABEmailTextField.h"
#import "EMABPasswordTextField.h"
#import "EMABUser.h"
@interface EMABSignupViewController ()<UITableViewDataSource, UITableViewDelegate,
UITextFieldDelegate>
@property (nonatomic, strong) EMABEmailTextField *emailTextField;
@property (nonatomic, strong) EMABPasswordTextField *passwordTextField;
@property (nonatomic, strong) EMABPasswordTextField *passwordAgainTextField;
@end
```

You also need to create three properties to reference EMABEmailTextField and EMABPasswordTextfield. Since you still want to give some room to display each cell's title, you want to size and position each UITextField. The following code shows how to do that using the -(void) viewDidLoad method.

```objc
- (void)viewDidLoad {
    [super viewDidLoad];

    self.emailTextField = [[EMABEmailTextField alloc] initWithFrame:CGRectMake(kLeftMargin,
    kTopMargin, kTextFieldWidth, kTextFieldHeight)];
    self.emialTextField.delegate = self;
    self.passwordTextField = [[EMABPasswordTextField alloc] initWithFrame:CGRectMake
    (kLeftMargin, kTopMargin, kTextFieldWidth, kTextFieldHeight)];
    self.passwordTextField.delegate = self;
    self.passwordAgainTextField = [[EMABPasswordTextField alloc] initWithFrame:
    CGRectMake(kLeftMargin, kTopMargin, kTextFieldWidth, kTextFieldHeight)];
    [self.passwordAgainTextField setPlaceholder:NSLocalizedString(@"Password Again",
    @"Password Again")];
    self.passwordAgainTextField.delegate = self;
}
```

Keep in mind that kLeftMargin, kTopMargin, kTextFieldWidth, and kTextFieldHeight are defined in the EMABConstants class. You will need them again in other instances.

Next, move to the implementation of UITableViewDataSource methods. You need one section and three cells for this UITableView.

```objc
#pragma mark - tableview datasource
-(NSInteger)tableView:(UITableView *)tableView numberOfRowsInSection:(NSInteger)section
{
    return 3;
}
-(NSInteger)numberOfSectionsInTableView:(UITableView *)tableView
{
    return 1;
}
```

Having set the identifier "SignUpCell" in the nib file on UIStoryboard, here is how you create three cells:

```objc
-(UITableViewCell *)tableView:(UITableView *)tableView cellForRowAtIndexPath:(NSIndexPath *)
indexPath
{
    UITableViewCell *cell = nil;

    cell = [tableView dequeueReusableCellWithIdentifier:@"SignupCell"
    forIndexPath:indexPath];

    UITextField *textField = nil;
    switch (indexPath.row) {
        case 0:
            textField = self.emailTextField;
            break;
        case 1:
            textField = self.passwordTextField;
            break;
```

```
        case 2:
            textField = self.passwordAgainTextField;
            break;
        default:
            break;
    }

    // make sure this textfield's width matches the width of the cell
    CGRect newFrame = textField.frame;
    newFrame.size.width = CGRectGetWidth(cell.contentView.frame) - kLeftMargin*2;
    textField.frame = newFrame;

    // if the cell is ever resized, keep the textfield's width to match the cell's width
    textField.autoresizingMask = UIViewAutoresizingFlexibleWidth;

    [cell.contentView addSubview:textField];

    return cell;

}
```

The last piece is to handle one of the delegate methods of UITableView. You don't really have to implement it.

```
-(void)tableView:(UITableView *)tableView didSelectRowAtIndexPath:(NSIndexPath *)indexPath
{
    [tableView deselectRowAtIndexPath:indexPath animated:NO];
}
```

As you can see, it's pretty easy to set up your views. However, signing up a user requires a little bit of extra work.

First, you need to check whether the user provides a valid e-mail address. You can use the -(BOOL)isValidEmail method:

```
#pragma mark - helper
-(BOOL)isValidEmail {
    //https://github.com/benmcredmond/DHValidation
    NSString *emailRegex = @"[A-Z0-9a-z._%+-]+@[A-Za-z0-9.-]+\\.[A-Za-z]{2,6}";
    NSPredicate *emailTest = [NSPredicate predicateWithFormat:@"SELF MATCHES %@", emailRegex];
    return [emailTest evaluateWithObject:self.emailTextField.text];
}
```

Next, you want to remind the user when there is something wrong with the e-mail entered; use UIAlertView for this. Later you will also show other alert information such as the password length or sign-up errors. Let's create a -(void)showWarning:(NSString *)message helper method:

```
-(void)showWarning:(NSString *)message {
    [[[UIAlertView alloc] initWithTitle:NSLocalizedString(@"Warning", @"Warning")
    message:message delegate:nil cancelButtonTitle:NSLocalizedString(@"OK", @"OK")
    otherButtonTitles:nil , nil] show];
}
```

Lastly, you also want to allow the user to dismiss the software keyboard, so you implement the UITextField delegate method as follows:

```
#pragma mark - UITextField Delegate
-(BOOL)textFieldShouldReturn:(UITextField *)textField
{
    [textField resignFirstResponder];
    return YES;
}
@end
```

Next, implement the IBAction when a user taps the "Sign Up" button. Check whether the two password UITextField cells meet the minimum text length requirements; and whether the two text fields have identical text. Also make sure the text length in Email UITextField meets the requirement of minimum text length and is a valid e-mail address. If something is wrong with the information entered, the related warning will be provided afterward. Lastly, use [PFUser user] to create a user instance and cast it to the EMABUser. The username and e-mail of this user are the text in the e-mail UITextField text, and the password of the user is the text in the password UITextfield cell; then you use the Parse -(BFTask *) signUpInBackground method. Here is the complete implementation:

```
-(IBAction)onSignup:(id)sender{
    BOOL cont0 = [self.passwordTextField.text length] > kMinTextLength;
    BOOL cont1 = [self.passwordAgainTextField.text length] > kMinTextLength;
    BOOL cont2 = [self.passwordTextField.text isEqualToString:
                self.passwordAgainTextField.text];
    BOOL cont3 = [self.emailTextField.text length] > kMinTextLength;
    BOOL cont4 = [self isValidEmail];

    if (!cont0) {
        [self showWarning:NSLocalizedString(@"Password at least 6 characters.", @"Password
        at least 6 characters.")];
    }
    if (!cont1) {
        [self showWarning:NSLocalizedString(@"Password at least 6 characters.", @"Password
        at least 6 characters.")];
    }
    if (!cont2) {
        [self showWarning:NSLocalizedString(@"Passwords have to match.", @"Passwords have to
        match.")];
    }
    if (!cont3) {
        [self showWarning:NSLocalizedString(@"Email at least 6 characters.", @"Password at
        least 6 characters.")];
    }

    if (!cont4) {
        [self showWarning:NSLocalizedString(@"Doesn't look like a valid email.", @"Doesn't
        look like a valid email.")];
    }
```

```
    if (cont0 && cont1 && cont2 && cont3 && cont4) {
        [self.emailTextField resignFirstResponder];
        [self.passwordTextField resignFirstResponder];
        [self.passwordAgainTextField resignFirstResponder];
        EMABUser *user = (EMABUser *)[PFUser user];
        user.username = [self.emailTextField text];
        user.email = [self.emailTextField text];
        user.password = [self.passwordTextField text];
        [user signUpInBackgroundWithBlock:^(BOOL succeeded, NSError *error){
            if (!error) {
                [self dismissViewControllerAnimated:YES completion:nil];
            }
        }];
    }
}
```

Summary

This chapter explained how to create a user interface (UI) to let a user sign up for an account with an e-mail and password. It also covered how to develop a better user experience while developing the UI. In the end, signing a user up with Parse is just an API method.

Chapter 9

The Login Feature

In the previous chapter, you learned how to sign up new users. In this chapter, you will learn how to implement the log in and log in with Facebook features.

Using Direct Log In

Similar to the sign-up feature, the user logs in with an e-mail and password, so you can use the same model (EMABUser), similar views (EMABEmailTextField, EMABPasswordTextField, and UITableView), and a "Log In" button.

Before requesting Parse to verify the information a user provides, you need to do some information check as you have done for the sign-up feature; for example, you need to check whether the e-mail is valid, the e-mail length meets the minimum length requirement, and the password length meets the minimum length requirement. You also need to set up some helper methods, one will repeat the e-mail verification method. For this reason, you move this method to EMABConstants.

The key Login API from Parse is + (void)logInWithUsernameInBackground:(NSString *) username password:(NSString *)password block:(PF_NULLABLE PFUserResultBlock)block.

Here is the implementation:

EMABLoginViewController.m

```
#import "EMABLoginViewController.h"
#import "EMABConstants.h"
#import "EMABUser.h"
#import "EMABEmailTextField.h"
#import "EMABPasswordTextField.h"
@interface EMABLoginViewController ()<UITableViewDataSource, UITableViewDelegate,
UITextFieldDelegate>
@property (nonatomic, strong) UITextField *emailTextField;
@property (nonatomic, strong) UITextField *passwordTextField;
@property (nonatomic, weak) IBOutlet UITableView *loginTableView;
@end
```

```objc
@implementation EMABLoginViewController
- (void)viewDidLoad {
    [super viewDidLoad];
    self.emailTextField = [[EMABEmailTextField alloc] initWithFrame:CGRectMake(kLeftMargin,
    kTopMargin, kTextFieldWidth, kTextFieldHeight)];
    self.emailTextField.delegate = self;
    self.passwordTextField = [[EMABPasswordTextField alloc] initWithFrame:CGRectMake
    (kLeftMargin, kTopMargin, kTextFieldWidth, kTextFieldHeight)];
    self.passwordTextField.delegate = self;
}

-(IBAction)onLogin:(id)sender{

    BOOL cont0 = [self.passwordTextField.text length] > kMinTextLength;
    BOOL cont1 = [self.emailTextField.text length] > kMinTextLength;
    BOOL cont2 = [EMABConstants isValidEmail:self.emailTextField.text];

    if (!cont0) {
        [self showWarning:NSLocalizedString(@"Password at least 6 characters.",
        @"Password at least 6 characters.")];
    }

    if (!cont1) {
        [self showWarning:NSLocalizedString(@"Email at least 6 characters.",
        @"Password at least 6 characters.")];
    }

    if (!cont2) {
        [self showWarning:NSLocalizedString(@"Doesn't look like a valid email.",
        @"Doesn't look like a valid email.")];
    }

    if (cont0 && cont1 && cont2) {
        [self.emailTextField resignFirstResponder];
        [self.passwordTextField resignFirstResponder];

        [PFUser logInWithUsernameInBackground:self.emailTextField.text password:self.
        passwordTextField.text
                        block:^(PFUser *user, NSError *error) {
                            if (!error) {
                                [self dismissViewControllerAnimated:YES completion:nil];
                            } else {
                                [self showWarning:[error localizedDescription]];
                            }
                        }];
    }

}
```

```objc
#pragma mark - tableview datasource
-(NSInteger)tableView:(UITableView *)tableView numberOfRowsInSection:(NSInteger)section
{
    return 2;
}
-(NSInteger)numberOfSectionsInTableView:(UITableView *)tableView
{
    return 1;
}

-(UITableViewCell *)tableView:(UITableView *)tableView cellForRowAtIndexPath:(NSIndexPath *)
indexPath
{
    UITableViewCell *cell = nil;

    cell = [tableView dequeueReusableCellWithIdentifier:@"LoginCell" forIndexPath:indexPath];

    UITextField *textField = nil;
    switch (indexPath.row) {
        case 0:
            textField = self.emailTextField;
            break;
        case 1:
            textField = self.passwordTextField;
            break;
        default:
            break;
    }

    // make sure this textfield's width matches the width of the cell
    CGRect newFrame = textField.frame;
    newFrame.size.width = CGRectGetWidth(cell.contentView.frame) - kLeftMargin*2;
    textField.frame = newFrame;

    // if the cell is ever resized, keep the textfield's width to match the cell's width
    textField.autoresizingMask = UIViewAutoresizingFlexibleWidth;

    [cell.contentView addSubview:textField];

    return cell;

}

-(void)tableView:(UITableView *)tableView didSelectRowAtIndexPath:(NSIndexPath *)indexPath
{
    [tableView deselectRowAtIndexPath:indexPath animated:NO];
}
```

```
#pragma mark - helper
-(void)showWarning:(NSString *)message {
    [[[UIAlertView alloc] initWithTitle:NSLocalizedString(@"Warning", @"Warning")
    message:message delegate:nil cancelButtonTitle:NSLocalizedString(@"OK", @"OK")
    otherButtonTitles:nil , nil] show];
}

#pragma mark - UITextField Delegate
-(BOOL)textFieldShouldReturn:(UITextField *)textField
{
    [textField resignFirstResponder];
    return YES;
}

@end
```

Using Facebook Login

It's quite typical for an iOS e-commerce app to integrate Facebook Login for Apps. Although it can be challenging to manage two sets of users, the Facebook SDK can be used together with the Parse SDK, and is integrated with the PFUser class to make linking users to their Facebook identities easy.

This feature requires the ParseFacebookUtilities SDK, so you need to modify your Podfile as follows:

```
pod 'ParseFacebookUtilsV4','1.7.1'
```

> **Note**   Facebook and Parse change their SDKs frequently. You may need to update the SDK version by the time you run this demo.

In this section, you learn how to implement Facebook Login with Parse, as well as how to obtain the user's Facebook profile so you can save it for your own records.

Remember that you will need a Facebook Developer account for implementing this feature (see Chapter 4 for details).

For the model, use EMABUser (the same model as in Chapter 8); for the view, use the "Log In with Facebook" button (see Chapter 8). Since you need to talk to the Facebook API to authorize the user, you also need to obtain the user's profile and save it to the Parse back end. I will introduce a UIActivityIndicator to indicate the ongoing process, and also disable some buttons in case users don't want to wait until finished. The whole idea is to create a friendlier user experience.

Here is the header declaration:

```
#import "EMABDispatchViewController.h"
#import "EMABConstants.h"
#import "EMABUser.h"
```

```
#import <ParseFacebookUtils/PFFacebookUtils.h>
@interface EMABDispatchViewController ()
@property (nonatomic, weak) IBOutlet UIActivityIndicatorView *activityIndicatorView;
@end
```

When a user sees this screen, the c instance is hidden. Only when a user taps the "Log In with Facebook" button and a network request is made will it be visible. Once the network request is finished, the animation stops and the UIActivityIndicator instance is hidden.

```
@implementation EMABDispatchViewController

- (void)viewDidLoad {
    [super viewDidLoad];
    self.activityIndicatorView.hidden = YES;

}
```

The helper method -(void)updateIndicator updates the UI. When making a Facebook API request, you want to disable the left bar button item to prevent the user from skipping the login process. You also use this method to show or hide the indicator.

```
-(void)updateIndicator:(BOOL)shouldEnable{
    self.navigationItem.leftBarButtonItem.enabled = !shouldEnable;
    (shouldEnable)?[self.activityIndicatorView startAnimating]:[self.activityIndicatorView
    stopAnimating];
    self.activityIndicatorView.hidden = !shouldEnable;

}
```

As you have done in previous chapters, use UIAlertView to show any error that might occur during the login process.

```
#pragma mark - helper
-(void)showError:(NSString *)message {
    [[[UIAlertView alloc] initWithTitle:NSLocalizedString(@"Error", @"Error")
    message:message delegate:nil cancelButtonTitle:NSLocalizedString(@"OK", @"OK")
    otherButtonTitles:nil , nil] show];
}
```

Next, move to the Facebook login process. First, tell Facebook what information is obtained from the user, and ask permission from Facebook. In this case, you only need some basic information "user_about_me" such as the user's e-mail, name, and gender. If you need more information, you need to log in to the developer.facebook.com portal to request additional permission.

Once again, Parse makes this process easy. You will use the PFFacebookUtils method logInWithPermissions:block to make this request.

When you make this request, you might get a success or an error message. If you get an error, you can simply let the user know there is something wrong and indicate what is wrong. You use the showError: method for this purpose. When you get a success, you will get a PFUser instance. But there is no Facebook user information associated with this PFUser instance; this requires an extra step. That's why you need another helper method, obtainFacebookUserInfo:

```
-(IBAction)onFacebookLogin:(id)sender{
    // Set permissions required from the facebook user account
    NSArray *permissionsArray = @[@"user_about_me"];
    [self updateIndicator:YES];
    [PFFacebookUtils logInWithPermissions:permissionsArray block:^(PFUser *user, NSError
    *error) {
        if (error) {
                NSString *facebookError = [FBErrorUtility userMessageForError:error];
                [self showError:facebookError];
            } else {
                [self obtainFacebookUserInfo:user];
        }
        [self updateIndicator:NO];
    }];
}
```

To start requesting this user's Facebook profile information, you use [FBRequest requestForMe] to create a FBRequest instance as shown in the following code. The next method is the FBRequest instance method, startWithCompletionHandler. This asynchronous callback will return either an error or the result you are looking for. Similarly, you can handle any error by showing it to the user; in the meantime, leave this screen, and return to the main app. You don't want the user to get stuck here.

If you receive a successful result, you will map this dictionary result to the EMABUser instance properties. As mentioned before, the "user_about_me" permission will get you information about the user such as e-mail, name, gender, and profile image url. It's easy to map the e-mail, name, and gender.

```
NSDictionary *userData = (NSDictionary *)result;
 [fbUser setEmail:userData[@"email"]];
 [fbUser setUsername:userData[@"email"]];
 [fbUser setName:userData[@"name"]];
 if (userData[@"gender"]) {
                [fbUser setGender:userData[@"gender"]];
 }
```

Mapping the image URL to PFFile as declared in EMABUser requires some additional work. First, you need to get the image URL in the correct format.

```
NSString *facebookID = userData[@"id"];
            NSURL *pictureURL = [NSURL URLWithString:[NSString stringWithFormat:
            @"https://graph.facebook.com/%@/picture?type=square&return_ssl_resources=1",
            facebookID]];
```

In this case, you use the user's square profile picture. To transform from an image URL to PFFile, you can get the NSData from this URL, then use the [PFFile fileWithName:Data] class method to create a PFFile instance. The following code shows how to approach this problem:

```
if ([pictureURL absoluteString]) {
                dispatch_queue_t queue = dispatch_get_global_queue(DISPATCH_QUEUE_PRIORITY_
                HIGH, 0ul);
                dispatch_async(queue, ^{
                    NSData * imageData = [NSData dataWithContentsOfURL:[NSURL
                    URLWithString:[pictureURL absoluteString]]];
                    dispatch_async(dispatch_get_main_queue(), ^{
                        PFFile *iconFile = [PFFile fileWithName:@"avatar.jpg"
                        data:imageData];
                        [iconFile saveInBackgroundWithBlock:^(BOOL succeeded, NSError
                        *error) {
                            if (!error) {
                                fbUser.photo = iconFile;
                            }
                        }];

                    });
                });
        }
```

Finally, you save this EMABUser instance and dismiss the current screen:

```
[fbUser saveInBackgroundWithBlock:^(BOOL succeeded, NSError *error) {
                if (!error) {
                    [self dismissViewControllerAnimated:YES completion:nil];
                }
}];
```

Here is the complete implementation:

```
-(void)obtainFacebookUserInfo:(PFUser *)user{
    [self updateIndicator:YES];
    EMABUser *fbUser = (EMABUser *)user;
    FBRequest *request = [FBRequest requestForMe];
    [request startWithCompletionHandler:^(FBRequestConnection *connection, id result,
    NSError *error) {
        [self updateIndicator:NO];
        if (!error) {
            // Parse the data received

            NSString *facebookID = userData[@"id"];
            NSURL *pictureURL = [NSURL URLWithString:[NSString stringWithFormat:
            @"https://graph.facebook.com/%@/picture?type=square&return_ssl_resources=1",
            facebookID]];
```

```
            if ([pictureURL absoluteString]) {
                dispatch_queue_t queue = dispatch_get_global_queue(DISPATCH_QUEUE_PRIORITY_
                HIGH, 0ul);
                dispatch_async(queue, ^{
                    NSData * imageData = [NSData dataWithContentsOfURL:[NSURL
                    URLWithString:[pictureURL absoluteString]]];
                    dispatch_async(dispatch_get_main_queue(), ^{
                        PFFile *iconFile = [PFFile fileWithName:@"avatar.jpg"
                        data:imageData];
                        [iconFile saveInBackgroundWithBlock:^(BOOL succeeded, NSError
                        *error) {
                            if (!error) {
                                fbUser.photo = iconFile;
                            }
                        }];

                    });
                });
            }

            [fbUser saveInBackgroundWithBlock:^(BOOL succeeded, NSError *error) {
                if (!error) {
                    [self dismissViewControllerAnimated:YES completion:nil];
                }
            }];

        } else if ([[[[error userInfo] objectForKey:@"error"] objectForKey:@"type"]
                isEqualToString: @"OAuthException"]) {
            [self dismissViewControllerAnimated:YES completion:^{
                [self showError:@"The facebook session was invalidated"];
            }];
        } else {
            [self dismissViewControllerAnimated:YES completion:^{
                [self showError:[error localizedDescription]];
            }];
        }
    }];
}

-(IBAction)onCancel:(id)sender{
    [self dismissViewControllerAnimated:YES completion:nil];
}

@end
```

Summary

In this chapter I explained how to log in a registered user while providing an intuitive and friendly user experience. I also covered how to implement Facebook Login with Apps, obtain a user's Facebook profile, and then save the information to the Parse backend by incorporating the Parse ParseFacebookUtilsV4 SDK.

Chapter 10

Shopping Bag

At this point, if you followed along, you have a registered user who is ready to add products into his or her shopping bag. In this chapter, I show you how to add a product to the shopping bag, update the product's quantity, delete an individual product or all of them from the bag, and update the total amount. The customer should be able to see what's in the bag when he or she returns to it.

Shopping Bag Model

First, the model to represent an item in a shopping bag: create a PFObject subclass, and name it EMABOrderItem. Then register this class name with EMABConstant by giving it an NSString key: kOrderItem. This subclass has two properties: one is the quantity, and the other is an EMABProduct instance. Also create an instance method -(double)subTotal to calculate the total amount of this item.

Here is the header file:

EMABOrderItem.h

```
#import <Parse/Parse.h>
@class EMABProduct;

@interface EMABOrderItem : PFObject
@property (nonatomic, assign) double quantity;
@property (nonatomic, strong) EMABProduct *product;

-(double)subTotal;
@end
```

In the implementation file, the subTotal method simply returns the multiple(s) of quantity and this product's unit price.

Here is the implementation code:

EMABOrderItem.m

```
#import "EMABOrderItem.h"
#import  <Parse/PFObject+Subclass.h>
#import "EMABConstants.h"
#import "EMABProduct.h"
@implementation EMABOrderItem
@dynamic quantity,product;
+(NSString *)parseClassName
{
    return kOrderItem;
}


-(double)subTotal {
    return self.quantity *self.product.unitPrice;
}

@end
```

The second model you need is the EMABOrder model; register an NSString key with the EMABConstants class called: kOrder.

Don't forget, you also need to register these two PFObject subclasses with your AppDelegate.

For this model class, you need a few properties: the user, all order items, an order number (that you will assign), the order date, and an order status. The order status enum type is how you distinguish whether an order is in the shopping bag or has been processed. To make it readable, the enum type is declared in the EMABConstants class.

```
typedef NS_OPTIONS(NSInteger, ORDER_STATUS){
    ORDER_NOT_MADE = 0,
    ORDER_MADE = 1
};
```

You also need some helper methods: one to display the total amount in the bag; one is, obviously, your `basicQuery` method; one to query for a user; and one to query for a user with an order status.

Here is the header file:

EMABOrder.h

```
#import <Parse/Parse.h>
#import "EMABConstants.h"
@class EMABOrderItem;
@class EMABUser;
@interface EMABOrder : PFObject<PFSubclassing>
@property (nonatomic, strong) EMABUser *customer;
```

```
@property (nonatomic, assign) int64_t orderNo;
@property (nonatomic, assign) NSDate *orderDate;
@property (nonatomic, strong) NSArray *items;
@property (nonatomic, assign) ORDER_STATUS orderStatus;

-(double)total;
+(PFQuery *)basicQuery;
+(PFQuery *)queryForCustomer:(EMABUser *)customer;
+(PFQuery *)queryForCustomer:(EMABUser *)customer orderStatus:(ORDER_STATUS)status;
@end
```

In the implementation, to calculate the total amount, you simply iterate each order item, and summarize the subtotal you have created in the OrderItem class.

```
-(double)total
{
    double sum = 0.0;
    if (self.items) {
        for (EMABOrderItem *item in self.items) {
            sum += [item subTotal];
        }
    }
    return sum;
}
```

In the +(PFQuery *)basicQuery method, you include the product in each OrderItem. Parse anticipates this use case, so it provides a dot notation for this purpose.

```
+(PFQuery *)basicQuery{
    PFQuery *query = [PFQuery queryWithClassName:[self parseClassName]];
    [query includeKey:@"items.product"];
    [query orderByDescending:@"createdAt"];
    return query;
}
```

Remember to keep the name consistent. You have a property whose name is "items" that is an array of EMABOrderItem instances. An EMABOrderItem has the "product" property. To make the dot notation work properly, "items" and "product" should be used.

The +(PFQuery *)queryForCustomer:(EMABUser *)customer method is implemented based on the basicQuery method; you only need to add the following statement:

```
[query whereKey:@"customer" equalTo:customer];
+(PFQuery *)queryForCustomer:(EMABUser *)customer {
    PFQuery *query = [self basicQuery];
    [query whereKey:@"customer" equalTo:customer];
    return query;
}
```

Likewise, +(PFQuery *)queryForCustomer:(EMABUser *)customer orderStatus:(ORDER_
STATUS)status is based on +(PFQuery *)queryForCustomer:(EMABUser *)customer:

```
+(PFQuery *)queryForCustomer:(EMABUser *)customer orderStatus:(ORDER_STATUS)status{
    PFQuery  *query = [self queryForCustomer:customer];
    [query whereKey:@"orderStatus" equalTo:@(status)];
    return query;
}
```

These are all you need for now. Any other methods you may need can be added to this model class later.

Shopping Bag View

One of the important views for this shopping bag is the item UITableViewCell, shown in Figure 10-1.

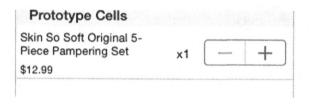

Figure 10-1. An order item cell

The cell consists of a UILabel to show the product name, a UILabel to show the unit price, a UILabel to show the quantity, and a UIStepper to give users the opportunity to change the quantity of the item they want to purchase.

The layout of these UI elements is simple and straightforward. Create a PFTableViewCell subclass, and name it EMABOrderItemTableViewCell. Here is the header file:

EMABOrderItemTableViewCell.h

```
#import "PFTableViewCell.h"
@class EMABOrderItem;
@interface EMABOrderItemTableViewCell : PFTableViewCell
-(void)configureItem:(EMABOrderItem *)item;
@end
```

The instance method -(void)configureItem in this header file works as previously described.

Below is the implementation file of this class:

EMABOrderItemTableViewCell.m

```
#import "EMABOrderItemTableViewCell.h"
#import "EMABOrderItem.h"
#import "EMABProduct.h"
@interface EMABOrderItemTableViewCell()
```

```
@property (nonatomic, weak) IBOutlet UILabel *nameLabel;
@property (nonatomic, weak) IBOutlet UILabel *unitPriceLabel;
@property (nonatomic, weak) IBOutlet UILabel *quantityLabel;
@property (nonatomic, weak) IBOutlet UIStepper *quantityStepper;
@end

@implementation EMABOrderItemTableViewCell
-(void)configureItem:(EMABOrderItem *)item {
    self.nameLabel.text = item.product.name;
    self.unitPriceLabel.text = [item.product friendlyPrice];
    self.quantityLabel.text = [item friendlyQuantity];
}
@end
```

Basically, you rely on the xib file and use IBOutlet to instantiate the UI elements. You use the configureItem method to display item information such as product name, price, and quantity.

Shopping Bag Controller

Recall that in Chapter 7 I instructed you to add a to-do comment for the routine that enables you to add an item to the shopping bag:

```
-(IBAction)onBag:(id)sender
{
    if ([PFAnonymousUtils isLinkedWithUser:[PFUser currentUser]]) {
        [self showWarning];
    } else {
        //todo:
    }

}
```

Now it's time to complete this feature.

For me personally, I want this experience to be as simple as possible. If "Add to Bag" is tapped, the item is silently added to the shopping bag and the user is informed that the item has been added. The user won't be able to specify the quantity during this process; users can change the quantity before checkout. You don't want to implement the identical features at two different places.

You need to handle two different use cases:

- The shopping bag is empty. In this case, you create a new EMABOrderItem and EMABOrder instance.

- The shopping bag is not empty. In this case, you need to query the Parse back end. First, query the back end to see whether the user has an unfinished order. If so, create a local EMABOrder instance to keep track of it. On second thought, there will be two cases after the user taps "Add to the Bag": (1) the existing order doesn't contain this product; (2) the user might have the same item in the bag already, and now we interpret it that the user wants to add the same item again.

With this in mind, add the following property to the EMABProductDetailViewController class:

```
@property(nonatomic, strong) EMABOrder *order;
```

Set up a helper method `-(void)queryForUnfinishedOrder`.

```
-(void)queryForUnfinishedOrder{
    PFQuery *orderQuery = [EMABOrder queryForCustomer:[EMABUser currentUser]
    orderStatus:ORDER_NOT_MADE];

    __weak typeof(self) weakSelf = self;
    [orderQuery getFirstObjectInBackgroundWithBlock:^(PFObject *order, NSError *error){
        if (!error) {
            weakSelf.order = (EMABOrder *)order;
        }
    }];
}
```

Also create a helper method to check whether an order items array contains a product. Basically, you iterate this array and check the objectId property of this product. Here is the code:

```
-(int)containsProduct:(NSArray *)items target:(EMABProduct *)product {
    int index = -1;
    for (int i = 0; i<[items count]; i++){
        EMABOrderItem *item = items[i];
        if ([item.product.objectId isEqualToString:self.product.objectId]) {
            index = i;
            break;
        }
    }

    return index;
}
```

EMABOrder has an items property that is an array of EMABOrderItem instances. When adding a product to this order, you need to consider the following steps:

1.   Create an instance of EMABOrderItem. Let the product be the product currently viewed, and set the quantity to 1.

2.   Get the items array from the order instance. If it's null, create a new NSArray with the item from step 1. Let this NSArray instance be the items of this order. If it's not null, create a mutable copy of the items, and add a new element that is from step 1. Then give the immutable copy to this order as its items.

Create a helper method in the EMBAOrder class, and name it `-(void)addSingleProduct:(EMABProduct *)product`

```
-(void)addSingleProduct:(EMABProduct *)product{
    EMABOrderItem *item = [EMABOrderItem object];
    [item setProduct:product];
    [item setQuantity:1];
```

```
    if (self.items) {
        NSMutableArray *existedItems = [self.items mutableCopy];
        [existedItems addObject:item];
        [self setItems:[existedItems copy]];
    } else
        [self setItems:@[item]];

}
```

Finally, it's time to implement the onBag: IBAction method. Follow this logic sequence:

1. Do you have a registered user? If not, show a warning to ask the user to register or log in.

2. Do you have an unfinished order? If not, create a new EMABOrder instance, set properties such as customer and orderStatus, and call the -(void)addSingleProduct method. If yes, check whether this unfinished order contains the product you want to add to the bag. If not, call -(void)addSingleProduct and all dirty work will be handled by this method. If affirmative, you need to find out which item has this product, change the item's quantity by adding 1, then replace the items with the new one. In the end, you save this order instance asynchronically and let the user know once the save is done.

Here is the code:

```
-(IBAction)onBag:(id)sender
{
    if (![PFUser currentUser]) {
        [self showWarning];
    } else {
        if (self.order) {
            if ([self.order.items count] > 0) {
                if ([self containsProduct:self.order.items target:self.product] > -1) {
                    int index = [self containsProduct:self.order.items target:self.product];
                    NSMutableArray *eItems = [NSMutableArray arrayWithArray:self.order.items];
                    EMABOrderItem *foundItem = eItems[index];
                    [foundItem setQuantity:foundItem.quantity+1];
                    [eItems replaceObjectAtIndex:index withObject:foundItem];
                    self.order.items = [eItems copy];
                } else {
                    [self.order addSingleProduct:self.product];
                }
            } else {
                [self.order addSingleProduct:self.product];
            }
        } else {
            self.order = [EMABOrder object];
            [self.order setCustomer:[EMABUser currentUser]];
            [self.order setOrderStatus:ORDER_NOT_MADE];
```

```
        [self.order addSingleProduct:self.product];

    }
  }
  [self.order saveInBackgroundWithBlock:^(BOOL success, NSError *error){
      if (!error) {
          [self showSuccess];
      }
  }];
}
```

This probably is the most complicated logic you have handled so far in this book. The user won't know anything about your implementation detail. What happens is that a pop-up shows "Successfully added" once after the user taps the "Add to Bag" button.

Nexy, the EMABBagTableViewController, which is a subclass of UITableViewController. Here is the header file:

```
#import <UIKit/UIKit.h>
@interface EMABBagTableViewController : UITableViewController
@end
```

Figure 10-2 shows what the Bag screen looks like.

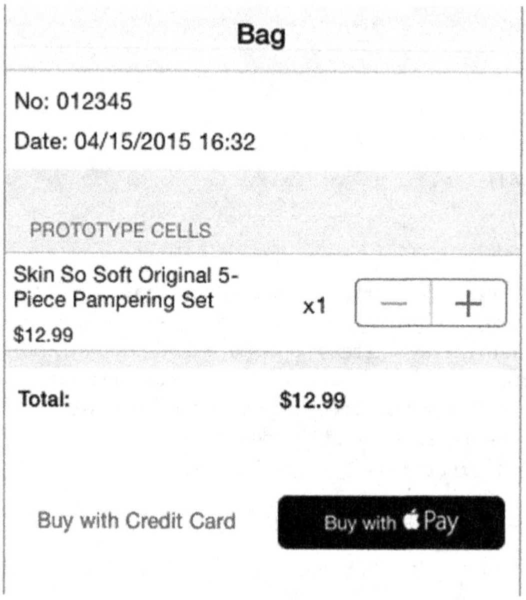

Figure 10-2. The Bag screen

You have already prepared EMABOrderItemTableViewCell for the UITableViewCell; you also need some other UI elements to show information such as order number, order date, total amount, and also the "Buy with Credit Card" and "Buy with Apple Pay" buttons.

You will use the UITableView header and footer views as the container views. The header view will be used to contain two UILabels: one UILabel shows the order number, the other UILabel shows the order date.

Think about the order number for a moment. You know the order number needs to be created on the the Parse back end. And an order can have an order number only if it has been placed successfully. In other words, you should not create an order number when the user only puts items in the shopping bag. So why do you create a UILabel for an order number? You can look at it in two ways. One is to show a "Your bag is empty" message as shown later. You can also reuse this screen to show an order detail after this user finishes the checkout process and wants to revisit the order details. (I will cover this scenario also in Chapter 16.)

The footer view of this UITableView contains two UILabels: One is for showing "Total:" text, the other is for showing the total amount in this bag. You also need two UIButtons: One is for checking out with a credit card, the other is for checking out with Apple Pay. As you can see, the UI layout itself is pretty straightforward.

Here is the EMABBagTableViewController header category:

```
@interface EMABBagTableViewController(){
}
@property (nonatomic, weak) IBOutlet UILabel *ordeNoLabel;
@property (nonatomic, weak) IBOutlet UILabel *ordeDateLabel;
@property (nonatomic, weak) IBOutlet UILabel *totalLabel;
@property (nonatomic, weak) IBOutlet UILabel *totalTextLabel;

@property (nonatomic, weak) IBOutlet UIButton *payWithCCButton;
@property (nonatomic, weak) IBOutlet UIButton *payWithApplePayButton;
@property (nonatomic, strong) EMABOrder *order;
@end
```

In the implementation, start from the -(void)viewWillAppear. As you have done in the EMABProductDetailViewController, query an unfinished order for this user.

```
-(void)viewWillAppear:(BOOL)animated
{
    [super viewWillAppear:animated];

    if ([EMABUser currentUser]) {
        [self queryForUnfinishedOrder];
    }
}
```

In the EMABOrder class, you have created the helper method queryForCustomer: orderStatus:. The customer will be the current EMABUser instance; the order status will be ORDER_NOT_MADE. To make the UI a little bit user-friendlier, you can take advantage of UIRefreshControl which you can specify through the nib file.

When making this query, we might or might not find something. If you don't get anything, you can assume that there is no pending order for this user, so you show a message to the user, and in the meantime hide all other UIs. You might need to keep doing this hiding and showing, depending on whether there is a pending order, or in case the user removes all items from the bag. For this purpose, create a helper method -(void)updateUI.

If there is no EMABorder instance or it's nil, hide everything else but the orderNo UILabel, and let this UILabel's text say "Your bag is empty." If there is an EMABOrder instance and it's not nil, you bring everything back. Here is the code:

```
-(void)updateUI {
    BOOL shouldClear = self.order == nil;
    if (shouldClear) {
        self.ordeNoLabel.text = NSLocalizedString(@"Your bag is empty.", @"");
        self.ordeDateLabel.text = @"";
        self.totalLabel.text = @"";
        self.totalTextLabel.text = @"";
        self.payWithApplePayButton.hidden = YES;
        self.payWithCCButton.hidden = YES;
        self.payWithApplePayButton.enabled = NO;
        self.payWithCCButton.enabled = NO;
    } else {
        self.totalTextLabel.text = NSLocalizedString(@"Total: ", @"");
        self.payWithApplePayButton.hidden = NO;
        self.payWithCCButton.hidden = NO;
        self.payWithApplePayButton.enabled = YES;
        self.payWithCCButton.enabled = YES;
    }
    [self.tableView reloadData];

}
```

Once this query returns a valid EMABOrder result, you show each piece of information such as the date the order is created and the total amount. Here is the complete code for this query:

```
-(IBAction)queryForUnfinishedOrder {
    self.order = nil; //to get ride of the cache
    PFQuery *orderQuery = [EMABOrder queryForCustomer:[EMABUser currentUser]
    orderStatus:ORDER_NOT_MADE];

    __weak typeof(self) weakSelf = self;
    [orderQuery getFirstObjectInBackgroundWithBlock:^(PFObject *order, NSError *error){
        if ([weakSelf.refreshControl isRefreshing]) {
            [weakSelf.refreshControl endRefreshing];
        }

        if (!error) {
            if (order) {
                weakSelf.order = (EMABOrder *)order;
                weakSelf.ordeNoLabel.text = @"";
                NSDateFormatter *dateFormatter = [[NSDateFormatter alloc] init];
```

```
                [dateFormatter setDateStyle:NSDateFormatterMediumStyle];
                [dateFormatter setTimeStyle:NSDateFormatterShortStyle];
                weakSelf.ordeDateLabel.text = [dateFormatter stringFromDate:[NSDate date]];
                weakSelf.totalLabel.text = [self.order friendlyTotal];
                [weakSelf updateUI];
            } else {
                [weakSelf updateUI];
            }
    } else {
            [weakSelf updateUI];
        }
    }];
}
```

You have a UITableView, and the item on the UITableView will be the order item. First, make the cell height a little taller than the default:

```
#pragma mark - UITableView Data Source
-(CGFloat)tableView:(UITableView *)tableView heightForRowAtIndexPath:(NSIndexPath *)
indexPath
{
    return 60.0;
}
```

There will be only one section:

```
- (NSInteger)numberOfSectionsInTableView:(UITableView *)tableView {
    return 1;
}
```

The total cell number is the items count in this order instance.

```
- (NSInteger)tableView:(UITableView *)tableView numberOfRowsInSection:(NSInteger)section {
    return [self.order.items count];
}
```

The cell itself will be an instance of EMABOrderItemTableViewCell. You probably noticed that I added a new parameter tag for this configureItem:(EMABOrderItem)item method. The reason is that you need to listen to which UIStepper is tapped. Provide a tag to keep track of it. The tag number will just be the row number.

```
- (EMABOrderItemTableViewCell*)tableView:(UITableView *)tableView cellForRowAtIndexPath:
(NSIndexPath *)indexPath {
    EMABOrderItemTableViewCell *cell = [tableView dequeueReusableCellWithIdentifier:
    @"BagItemCell" forIndexPath:indexPath];

    if (self.order) [cell configureItem:self.order.items[indexPath.row] tag:indexPath.row];
    else [cell configureItem:nil tag:100+indexPath.row];
    return cell;
}
```

Next, handle this while a user taps the UIStepper on any cell. When a user taps the UIStepper, it means the quantity of this item needs to be changed. "+" means increase by 1, "-" means subtract by 1. If the quantity is 0, remove the item from the order. If all items have 0 quantity, it means all items need to be removed.

With that logic in mind, create a mutable copy of the items of this order, then find the item you need to modify. It can be found by that tag index of the UIStepper this user taps.

However, you do want to alert this user when one is trying to reduce the quantity of the last or only item to 0. So you create a UIAlertController helper method called -(void) showDeleteAlert to let this user confirm. If the user confirms to do so, delete the order not only locally but also on the remote server. Once the order has been removed, perform another query -(void)queryForUnfinishedOrder to verify the deletion and also update the UI.

Here is the implementation:

```
-(void)showDeleteAlert {
    UIAlertController* alert = [UIAlertController alertControllerWithTitle:NSLocalizedString
    (@"Empty Bag",@"")
        message:NSLocalizedString(@"Are you sure you want to empty your bag?",@"")
        preferredStyle:UIAlertControllerStyleAlert];

    __weak typeof(self) weakSelf = self;
    UIAlertAction* defaultAction = [UIAlertAction actionWithTitle:NSLocalizedString
    (@"Yes",@"") style:UIAlertActionStyleDefault
        handler:^(UIAlertAction * action) {
            [weakSelf.order deleteInBackgroundWithBlock:^(BOOL success, NSError *error){
                if (!error) {
                    [weakSelf queryForUnfinishedOrder];
                }
            }];
        }];

    UIAlertAction* cancelAction = [UIAlertAction actionWithTitle:NSLocalizedString
    (@"cancel",@"") style:UIAlertActionStyleCancel
        handler:^(UIAlertAction * action) {}];

    [alert addAction:defaultAction];
    [alert addAction:cancelAction];
    [self presentViewController:alert animated:YES completion:nil];

}
```

Here is the -(IBAction)onStepper method—keep in mind that you always need to update the total amount whenever the user taps any UIStepper:

```
-(IBAction)onStepper:(id)sender {
    UIStepper *stepper = (UIStepper *)sender;
    NSInteger index = stepper.tag - 100;
    NSMutableArray *orderItems = [NSMutableArray arrayWithArray:self.order.items];
    EMABOrderItem *orderItem = orderItems[index];
    orderItem.quantity = (int)stepper.value;
```

```
    if ((int)stepper.value == 0) {
        [orderItems removeObjectAtIndex:index];
    } else {
        [orderItems replaceObjectAtIndex:index withObject:orderItem];
    }

    if ([orderItems count] == 0) {
        [self showDeleteAlert];
    } else {
        self.order.items = [orderItems copy];
        [self.tableView reloadData];
        self.totalLabel.text = [self.order friendlyTotal];
    }

}
```

What if the customer changed the quantity but doesn't check out yet? It is common that the user just likes exploring by moving things around. A customer may change the quantity in the bag, then leave the Bag screen to explore other product pages. In that case, save the order whenever the bag screen is about to disappear:

```
-(void)viewWillDisappear:(BOOL)animated
{
    if (self.order && self.order.isDirty) {
        [self.order saveInBackground];
    }
}
```

Here self.order.isDirty means the order has been changed.

Summary

This chapter covers the topic of how to implement a shopping bag and how to get it right for all kinds of use cases when dealing with customers and their shopping habits.

11

Shipping Address

In Chapter 10, you learned how to implement features such adding a product to the shopping bag, updating the product's quantity, deleting a product from the bag, and updating the total amount. In order for customers to complete the checkout process, however, you also need to collect additional information that you don't have yet: namely, the customer's shipping and billing addresses.

This chapter covers how to create a UITableView-based form to collect a US shipping address. The user interface itself might look pretty simple, but there are some tricks I need to cover.

Figure 11-1 shows what a shipping address form looks like.

Figure 11-1. The Shipping address form

Shipping Address Model

The model used in this chapter still is the EMABUser model, but you will need additional properties: address1, address2, city, state, and zip code. Here is the header file:

EMABUser.h

```
@interface EMABUser : PFUser<PFSubclassing>
@property (nonatomic, copy) NSString *firstName;
@property (nonatomic, copy) NSString *lastName;
@property (nonatomic, copy) NSString *name;
@property (nonatomic, copy) NSString *gender;
@property (nonatomic, copy) NSString *phone;
@property (nonatomic, copy) NSString *address1;
@property (nonatomic, copy) NSString *address2;
@property (nonatomic, copy) NSString *city;
@property (nonatomic, copy) NSString *state;
@property (nonatomic, copy) NSString *zipcode;
@property (nonatomic, copy) PFFile *photo;
```

Shipping Address View

Start by creating a UITableViewCell subclass, and name it EMABUserProfileTableViewCell. As you can see, a UITextField has been used on this cell. You also need a helper method to customize the cell's title, the UITextField's placeholder, and the keyboard type.

EMABUserProfileTableViewCell.h

```
@interface EMABUserProfileTableViewCell : UITableViewCell
@property (nonatomic, strong) UITextField *textField;
- (void)setContentForTableCellLabel:(NSString*)title placeHolder:(NSString *)placeHolder
text:(NSString *)text keyBoardType:(NSNumber *)type enabled:(BOOL)enabled;
@end
```

This time, you want to programmatically add this UITextField to this UITableViewCell as this cell's accessory view. You still have this cell set up on the xib file. So you need to call a different instantiation method, -(instancetype)initWithCoder:(NSCode *)aDecorder, as shown in the following code.

Keep in mind that you have used a constant value to position this UITextField. It won't work very well for different iPhone screen sizes. Since the focus in this book is really about the business logic, not the UI, this implementation might not fit all iPhone screen sizes.

Here is the instantiation method:

EMABUserProfileTableViewCell.m

```
@implementation EMABUserProfileTableViewCell

-(instancetype)initWithCoder:(NSCoder *)aDecoder
{
    self = [super initWithCoder:aDecoder];
    if (self) {
        self.textLabel.font = [UIFont boldSystemFontOfSize:14.0];
        CGRect frame = CGRectMake(100, kTopMargin, 210.0, kTextFieldHeight);
        self.textField = [[UITextField alloc] initWithFrame:frame];
        self.textField.borderStyle = UITextBorderStyleNone;
        self.textField.textColor = [UIColor blackColor];
        self.textField.font = [UIFont systemFontOfSize:13.0];
        self.textField.textAlignment = NSTextAlignmentRight;
        self.textField.contentVerticalAlignment = UIControlContentVerticalAlignmentCenter;
        self.textField.enabled = NO;
        self.textField.backgroundColor = [UIColor clearColor];
        self.textField.autocorrectionType = UITextAutocorrectionTypeNo;
        // no auto correction support
        self.textField.autocapitalizationType = UITextAutocapitalizationTypeWords;
        self.textField.returnKeyType = UIReturnKeyDone;
        self.textField.clearButtonMode = UITextFieldViewModeWhileEditing;
        // has a clear 'x' button to the right
```

```
        self.accessoryView = self.textField;
        self.selectionStyle = UITableViewCellSelectionStyleNone;
    }

    return self;
}
```

The helper method, -(void) - (void)setContentForTableCellLabel:(NSString*)title placeHolder:(NSString *)placeHolder :(NSString *)text keyBoardType:(NSNumber *) type enabled:(BOOL)enabled, is to use dynamic content to customize each cell. Here is its implementation:

```
- (void)setContentForTableCellLabel:(NSString*)title placeHolder:(NSString *)placeHolder
:(NSString *)text keyBoardType:(NSNumber *)type enabled:(BOOL)enabled
{
    self.textLabel.text = title;
    self.textField.text = text;
    self.textField.placeholder = placeHolder;
    self.textField.keyboardType = [type intValue];

    self.textField.layer.cornerRadius = 4.0f;
    self.textField.layer.masksToBounds = YES;
    self.textField.layer.borderColor = (enabled)?[[UIColor colorWithRed:0.0
    green:153.0/255.0 blue:204.0/255.0 alpha:1] CGColor ]:[[UIColor clearColor] CGColor];
    self.textField.layer.borderWidth = 1.0f;
    self.textField.enabled = enabled;

}
@end
```

This code also adds a border to the UITextField as shown in Figure 11-1.

Shipping Address Controller

In Xcode, create a new UITableViewController, and name it EMABUserProfileTableViewController.

EMABUserInfoViewController.m

```
#import "EMABUserProfileTableViewController.h"
#import "EMABUserProfileTableViewCell.h"
#import "EMABUser.h"
static NSString *kTitleKey = @"titleKey";
static NSString *kPlaceholderKey = @"placeholderKey";
static NSString *kKeyboardKey = @"keyboardTypeKey";

@interface EMABUserProfileTableViewController ()<UITextFieldDelegate>
@property (nonatomic, strong) NSArray *dataSourceArray;
@property (nonatomic, strong) EMABUser *customer;
@end
```

You have nine *static* UITableViewCells in this UITableView; that is, the titles of those cells are fixed, and the placeholder text of each UITextField in each cell is fixed. Instead of hard-coding them in each cell, use an NSArray to holder all contents, and assign to each cell dynamically. Each element in this NSArrray is an NSDictionary. Each dictionary has three keys. That's why the kTitleKey, kPlaceholderKey, and kKeyboardKey constants are defined in the static NSString.

You also defined an EMABUser property called customer. You need to use it to keep track of the user's input and keep consistent with this user.

Since there is a UITextField on each cell, you need to declare the UITextFieldDelegate in the interface category,

```
@interface EMABUserProfileTableViewController ()<UITextFieldDelegate>
```

EMABUserProfileTableViewController.m

```
@implementation EMABUserProfileTableViewController

- (void)viewDidLoad {
    [super viewDidLoad];
    self.dataSourceArray = @[
                        @{
                            kTitleKey:NSLocalizedString(@"First Name*", @"First Name"),
                            kPlaceholderKey:NSLocalizedString(@"First Name",
                            @"First Name"),
                            kKeyboardKey:@(UIKeyboardTypeNamePhonePad)},
                        @{
                            kTitleKey:NSLocalizedString(@"Last Name*",@""),
                            kPlaceholderKey:NSLocalizedString(@"Last Name",@""),
                            kKeyboardKey:@(UIKeyboardTypeNamePhonePad)},

                        @{
                            kTitleKey:NSLocalizedString(@"Phone*",@""),
                            kPlaceholderKey:@"555-555-5555",
                            kKeyboardKey:@(UIKeyboardTypePhonePad)},

                        @{
                            kTitleKey:NSLocalizedString(@"Email*",@""),
                            kPlaceholderKey:@"Email",
                            kKeyboardKey:@(UIKeyboardTypeEmailAddress)},

                        @{
                            kTitleKey:NSLocalizedString(@"Address 1*",@""),
                            kPlaceholderKey:@"Address 1",
                            kKeyboardKey:@(UIKeyboardTypeDefault)},
                        @{
                            kTitleKey:NSLocalizedString(@"Address 2",@""),
                            kPlaceholderKey:@"Address 2",
                            kKeyboardKey:@(UIKeyboardTypeDefault)},
```

```
                        @{
                            kTitleKey:NSLocalizedString(@"City*",@""),
                            kPlaceholderKey:NSLocalizedString(@"City",@""),
                            kKeyboardKey:@(UIKeyboardTypeDefault)},


                        @{
                            kTitleKey:NSLocalizedString(@"State*",@""),
                            kPlaceholderKey:NSLocalizedString(@"State",@""),
                            kKeyboardKey:@(UIKeyboardTypeDefault)},


                        @{
                            kTitleKey:NSLocalizedString(@"Zipcode*",@""),
                            kPlaceholderKey:@"#####",
                            kKeyboardKey:@(UIKeyboardTypeNumberPad)}
                        ];

    self.customer = [EMABUser currentUser];

}
```

Having set up the data source, you can add some real data to the UITableView. You have one section, nine cells - the size of dataSourceArray.

```
#pragma mark - Table view data source

- (NSInteger)numberOfSectionsInTableView:(UITableView *)tableView {
    return 1;
}

- (NSInteger)tableView:(UITableView *)tableView numberOfRowsInSection:(NSInteger)section {
    return [self.dataSourceArray count];
}

- (EMABUserProfileTableViewCell *)tableView:(UITableView *)tableView cellForRowAtIndexPath:
(NSIndexPath *)indexPath {
    EMABUserProfileTableViewCell *cell = [tableView dequeueReusableCellWithIdentifier:
    @"customerProfile" forIndexPath:indexPath];

    NSInteger row = indexPath.row;
    cell.textField.delegate = self;
    cell.textField.tag = 100 + row;

    NSString *text = @"";
    switch (row) {
```

```
        case 0:
            text = self.customer.firstName;
            break;
        case 1:
            text = self.customer.lastName;
            break;
        case 2:
            text = self.customer.phone;
            break;
        case 3:
            text = self.customer.email;
            break;
        case 4:
            text = self.customer.address1;
            break;
        case 5:
            text = self.customer.address2;
            break;
        case 6:
            text = self.customer.city;
            break;
        case 7:
            text = self.customer.state;
            break;
        case 8:
            text = self.customer.zipcode;
            break;
        default:
            break;
    }

    NSString *title = self.dataSourceArray[row][kTitleKey];
    NSString *placeholder = self.dataSourceArray[row][kPlaceholderKey];
    NSNumber *keyboardType = self.dataSourceArray[row][kKeyboardKey];

    [cell setContentForTableCellLabel:title placeHolder:placeholder text:text
    keyBoardType:keyboardType enabled:self.isEditing];
    return cell;
}
```

For each cell, the UITextField's text should be empty because the user has not entered anything. You probably also need to provide the option to let the user edit his or her address after entering all information. In other words, you will reuse the EMABUserProfileViewController on another occasion. That's why you let each UITextField's text correspond with one address property of the EMABUser model.

You also give each UITextField a tag that enables you to find out later which UITextField is being used.

Finally, customize each cell using the EMABUserProfileTableViewCell's helper method.

Next, implement the UITextField Delegate method.

```
#pragma mark - UITextField Delegate methods

- (BOOL)textFieldShouldBeginEditing:(UITextField *)textField
{
    return YES;
}

- (BOOL)textFieldShouldEndEditing:(UITextField *)textField
{
    switch (textField.tag) {
        case 100:
            self.customer.firstName = textField.text;
            break;
        case 101:
            self.customer.lastName = textField.text;
            break;
        case 102:
            self.customer.phone = textField.text;
            break;
        case 103:
            self.customer.email = textField.text;
            break;
        case 104:
            self.customer.address1 = textField.text;
            break;
        case 105:
            self.customer.address2 = textField.text;
            break;
        case 106:
            self.customer.city = textField.text;
            break;
        case 107:
            self.customer.state = textField.text;
            break;
        case 108:
            self.customer.zipcode = textField.text;
            break;
        default:
            break;
    }
    [textField resignFirstResponder];

    return YES;
}
- (BOOL)textFieldShouldReturn:(UITextField *)textField
{

    [textField resignFirstResponder];
    return YES;
}
```

The -(BOOL)textFieldShouldEndEditing:(UITextField *)textField is important. Once a user finishes a cell, you need to send the information to this user instance. It will be more obvious to see the reason when there are more cells, and a user has to scroll up and down to fill up the content.

As you can see, a "Done" bar button item is set up on the UINavigationBar. When the user taps "Done," whatever the user entered is saved and the screen is dimissed. But what if the user doesn't really enter anything, or the information provided is not sufficiently complete? Let's do a little check.

You need to declare a helper method in the header file of the EMABUser model:

```
-(BOOL)isShippingAddressCompleted;
```

Here is the implementation:

```
-(BOOL)isShippingAddressCompleted{
    BOOL cont0 = self.firstName && self.lastName && [self.firstName length] > 0 &&
    [self.lastName length] > 0;
    BOOL cont1 = self.address1 && [self.address1 length] > 0;
    BOOL cont2 = self.city && [self.city length] > 0;
    BOOL cont3 = self.state && [self.state length] > 0;
    BOOL cont4 = self.zipcode && [self.zipcode length]> 0;
    return cont0 && cont1 && cont1 && cont2 && cont3 && cont4;
}
```

Now you can use this helper method when the user taps "Done." If you think all information has been provided, save the user. If not, show an alert to notify the user that more information is needed.

```
-(IBAction)onDone:(id)sender
{
    [self.tableView.superview endEditing:YES];
    if ([self.customer isShippingAddressCompleted]) {
        __weak typeof(self) weakSelf = self;
        [self.customer saveInBackgroundWithBlock:^(BOOL succeeded, NSError *error) {
            if (!error) {
                [weakSelf.navigationController popViewControllerAnimated:YES];
            }
        }];
    } else {
        [SVProgressHUD showErrorWithStatus:NSLocalizedString(@"Please complete the required
        information denoted by *",@"")];
    }
}
```

Of course, you also provide a bar button item to let the user skip this screen.

```
-(void)onCancel:(id)sender
{
    [self.navigationController popViewControllerAnimated:YES];

}
```

That's all for this EMABUserProfileViewController. Return to EMABBagsTableViewController. When the user taps "Pay with Credit Card," we check whether the user has a complete shipping address:

```
-(IBAction)onPayWithCreditCard:(id)sender{
    if ([[EMABUser currentUser] isShippingAddressCompleted]) {
        //todo
    } else {
        EMABUserProfileTableViewController *viewController = [self.storyboard
        instantiateViewControllerWithIdentifier:@"EMABUserProfileTableViewController"];
        [self.navigationController pushViewController:viewController animated:YES];
    }

}
```

If the shipping address is incomplete, the EMABUserProfileTableViewController is presented. If the address is complete (YES), then you will ask for the user's credit card information—which is covered in the next chapter.

Summary

In this chapter, I covered how to use a UITableView to implement a form to collect a user's address. I used a UITableView to take advantage of the scrolling feature of a UITableView so a UITableViewCell can be moved to the screen top so the soft keyboard of a user's iPhone won't cover the content. I also considered different keyboard types for different address portions for easy typing purposes. There are definitely other ways to achieve the same goal. However, I feel my approach here is easier.

Chapter **12**

Pay with Credit Card

In the previous chapter, I talked about capturing a user's shipping address before checking out. In this chapter, I cover how a user can pay with a credit card. For this app, you will use the Stripe iOS SDK to make the process easier. To incorporate the Stripe iOS SDK, you need to update your Cocoapods Podfile by adding these two lines:

```
pod 'Stripe'
pod 'Stripe/ApplePay'
```

Then run "Pod update."

Payment Model

You need a new PFObject model for a user's credit card. Instead of naming it EMABCreditCard, name it EMABPaymentMethod because you might incorporate other payment methods such as PayPal in the future. Remember to register an NSString constant on the EMABConstants class and to register the model in the AppDelegate class.

In this model class, you need properties such as the owner of the payment method, the credit card type, the last four digits of the credit card, and the expiration month and year, as well as the Stripe Customer ID. You need the Stripe Customer ID property so you can ask Stripe to make a real charge against the credit card. You also need the Stripe Customer ID so that you can charge the same customer in the future without her having to reenter the same information.

In addition, you need some helper methods such as formatting the credit card's last four digits, the expiration month and year, and the credit card type (Visa, Master Card, etc.).

To get all credit cards for one customer, you need to perform a query. Like you have done before, you have a +(PFQuery *)basicQuery method, and the +(PFQuery *)queryForOwner: (EMABUser *)owner method.

Here is the header file:

EMABPaymentMethod.h

```
#import <Parse/Parse.h>
#import "Stripe.h"
@class EMABUser;
@interface EMABPaymentMethod : PFObject<PFSubclassing>
@property (nonatomic, copy) NSString *type;
@property (nonatomic, copy) NSString *stripeCustomerId;
@property (nonatomic, copy) NSString *lastFourDigit;
@property (nonatomic, assign) NSUInteger_t expirationMonth;
@property (nonatomic, assign) NSUInteger _t expirationYear;
@property (nonatomic, strong) EMABUser *owner;
-(NSString *)friendlyCreditCardNumber;
-(NSString *)friendlyExpirationMonthYear;
+(PFQuery *)basicQuery;
+(PFQuery *)queryForOwner:(EMABUser *)owner;
-(NSString *)friendlyType:(STPCardBrand)brand;
@end
```

Here is the implementation file:

EMABPaymentMethod.m

```
#import "EMABPaymentMethod.h"
#import <Parse/PFObject+Subclass.h>
#import "EMABUser.h"
#import "EMABConstants.h"
@implementation EMABPaymentMethod
@dynamic type,lastFourDigit, expirationMonth, expirationYear,stripeCustomerId, owner;

+(NSString *)parseClassName
{
    return kPaymentMethod;
}

-(NSString *)friendlyCreditCardNumber{
    return  [NSString stringWithFormat:@"####-####-####-%@",self. lastFourDigit];
}

-(NSString *)friendlyExpirationMonthYear{
    return [NSString stringWithFormat:@"%lld/%lld",self.expirationMonth,
    self.expirationYear];
}

+(PFQuery *)basicQuery{
    PFQuery *query = [PFQuery queryWithClassName:[self parseClassName]];
    [query orderByDescending:@"createdAt"];
    return query;
}
```

```objc
+(PFQuery *)queryForOwner:(EMABUser *)owner{
    PFQuery *query = [self basicQuery];
    [query whereKey:@"owner" equalTo:owner];
    return query;
}

-(NSString *)friendlyType:(STPCardBrand)brand{
    NSString *title = @"";
    switch (brand) {
        case STPCardBrandVisa:
            title = @"Visa";
            break;
        case STPCardBrandAmex:
            title = @"American Express";
            break;
        case STPCardBrandMasterCard:
            title = @"MasterCard";
            break;
        case STPCardBrandDiscover:
            title = @"Discover";
            break;
        case STPCardBrandJCB:
            title = @"JCB";
            break;
        case STPCardBrandDinersClub:
            title = @"Dinner Club";
            break;
        default:
            title = @"Unknown";
            break;
    }
    return title;
}

@end
```

In this implementation, for the helper method `-(NSString *)friendlyCreditCardNumber`, it might be better that it is formatted based on different credit card types. For example, American Express credit cards are normally 15 digits instead of 16.

Payment View

The Stripe iOS SDK sample code provides a "PKView" that you need to include in your project. It's not part of the Stripe iOS SDK. Figure 12-1 shows what it looks like.

Figure 12-1. The PKView

Payment Controller

Next, create a new UIViewController subclass, EMABAddCreditCardViewController. When this view controller is presented from EMABBagTableViewController, you want the controller to send the Stripe Customer ID back to EMABBagTableViewController so you can charge the customer's credit card.

To help with the data passing between the two controllers, you can use either the delegate or block method. Block is the preferred approach because it makes the code both simple and readable.

Here is the header file of the EMABAddCreditCardViewController:

EMABAddCreditCardViewController.h

```
#import <UIKit/UIKit.h>
@class EMABAddCreditCardViewController;
typedef void (^AddCreditCardViewControllerDidFinish)(NSString *customerId);

@interface EMABAddCreditCardViewController : UIViewController
@property (nonatomic, copy) AddCreditCardViewControllerDidFinish finishBlock;
@end
```

In the implementation file, you want to take full advantage of PTKView. One important feature is the delegate method of this PTKView. We declare this delegate on our EMABAddCreditCardViewController category interface.

EMABAddCreditCardViewController.m

```
#import "EMABAddCreditCardViewController.h"
#import "Stripe.h"
#import "PTKView.h"
#import "EMABUser.h"
#import "EMABPaymentMethod.h"
@interface EMABAddCreditCardViewController ()<PTKViewDelegate>
@property (nonatomic, weak) IBOutlet PTKView *paymentView;
@end
```

You also need a bar button item as the right item of this UINavigationItem; give it the title "Authorize." If this user has not finished entering her credit card information, you disable the bar button item. On the other hand, enable this button so the user can tap to authorize the credit card information again with Stripe serve. The following two methods are used for this purpose:

```
- (void)viewDidLoad {
    [super viewDidLoad];
    self.navigationItem.leftBarButtonItem = [[UIBarButtonItem alloc] initWithBarButtonSystem
    Item:UIBarButtonSystemItemCancel target:self action:@selector(onCancel:)];
    self.navigationItem.rightBarButtonItem = [[UIBarButtonItem alloc] initWithTitle:
    NSLocalizedString(@"Authorize", @"") style:UIBarButtonItemStylePlain target:self
    action:@selector(onAuthorize:)];
}

- (void)paymentView:(PTKView *)paymentView withCard:(PTKCard *)card isValid:(BOOL)valid {
    // Enable save button if the Checkout is valid
    self.navigationItem.rightBarButtonItem.enabled = valid;
}
```

Next, implement the onAuthorize: method. The logic is as follows. From the PTKView, you obtain the credit number and the expiration date, then you send this information to Stripe for verification. If the credit card information is valid, Stripe will send you a token. In a typical case, you can just use this token to charge the credit card. If you want to charge the same credit card again in the future, you can save the token to the Parse back end server.

In general, it's safe and convenient to store a token. However, it's better to relate each charge to a Stripe Customer object. For this reason, you request a Stripe Customer ID instead of a token when authorizing a credit card; this enables you to save this customer ID to Parse and reuse the ID to charge this credit card in the future. On the Parse back end, anyone who accesses your control panel will only see a customer ID, not a charge token. I think this approach is even better.

But how do you create a Stripe Customer ID? You can use the Parse Cloud function. I will go into details about the Parse Cloud function in Chapter 14; for now, I pretend there is a cloud function named "createStripeCustomer" already implement; so just use this for right now.

Here is your flow:

1. Based on the user's credit card information, make Stripe API call to get a Stripe token for the credit card.

2. Based on the Stripe Token, call your Parse Cloud function to get a Stripe Customer ID.

3. Based on partial information of the user's credit card, and the Stripe Customer ID you received in Step 2, create an EMABPayment instance; map the last four digits, expiration month and year, and Stripe Customer ID with the instance properties. Save this instance to Parse.

4. Once you save successfully, leave this screen and return to EMABBagViewController with a Stripe Customer ID, and then use this ID to charge the card.

Here is the full code:

```objc
- (void)onAuthorize:(id)sender {
    if (![self.paymentView isValid]) {
        return;
    }

    STPCard *card = [[STPCard alloc] init];
    card.number = self.paymentView.card.number;
    card.expMonth = self.paymentView.card.expMonth;
    card.expYear = self.paymentView.card.expYear;
    card.cvc = self.paymentView.card.cvc;
    [[STPAPIClient sharedClient] createTokenWithCard:card
        completion:^(STPToken *token, NSError *error) {
            if (error) {
            } else {
                EMABUser *user = [EMABUser currentUser];
                NSDictionary *stripeCustomerDictionary = @{@"tokenId":token.tokenId,
                @"customerEmail":user.email
            };
                [PFCloud callFunctionInBackground:@"createStripeCustomer" withParameters:
                stripeCustomerDictionary block:^(NSString *customerId, NSError *error) {
                    if (!error) {
                        EMABPaymentMethod *creditCard = [EMABPaymentMethod object];
                        creditCard.owner  = user;
                        creditCard.stripeCustomerId = customerId;
                        creditCard.expirationMonth = card.expMonth;
                        creditCard.expirationYear = card.expYear;
                        creditCard.type = [creditCard friendlyType:card.brand];
                        creditCard.lastFourDigit = card.last4;
                        creditCard.stripeCustomerId = customerId;
                        [creditCard saveInBackgroundWithBlock:^(BOOL succeeded, NSError
                        *error) {
                            if (!error) {
                                [self readyToCharge:customerId];
                            }
                        }];
                    } else {

                    }
                }];
            }
        }];
}

-(void)readyToCharge:(NSString *)customerId {
    [self dismissViewControllerAnimated:YES completion:^{
        self.finishBlock(self, customerId);
    }];
}
```

You also need to provide a "Cancel" bar button item so a user can skip this screen:

```
- (void)onCancel:(id)sender {
    [self.navigationController popViewControllerAnimated:YES];
}
```

Basically, that's all for this EMABAddCreditCardViewController.

There is still some work left on EMABBagsTableViewController. After the user taps "Buy with Credit Card," you check whether there is a shipping address. If not, you bring up the EMABUserProfileTableViewController. If yes, you need to bring up the EMABAddCreditCardViewController. Here is the code:

```
-(IBAction)onPayWithCreditCard:(id)sender{
    if ([[EMABUser currentUser] isShippingAddressCompleted]) {
        EMABAddCreditCardViewController *viewController =
        (EMABAddCreditCardViewController *)[self.storyboard
        instantiateViewControllerWithIdentifier:@"EMABAddCreditCardViewController"];
        __weak typeof(self) weakSelf = self;
        viewController.finishBlock = ^(NSString *customerId){
            [weakSelf charge:customerId];
        };
        [self.navigationController pushViewController:viewController animated:YES];

    } else {
        EMABUserProfileTableViewController *viewController = [self.storyboard
        instantiateViewControllerWithIdentifier:@"EMABUserProfileTableViewController"];
        [self.navigationController pushViewController:viewController animated:YES];
    }
}
```

You might have noticed the charge: method that has yet to be implemented. I will cover this implementation in the next chapter.

Summary

In this chapter, I showed how to integrate Stripe iOS SDK to collect a user's credit card information, authorize a charge, request a Stripe Customer ID, and save the ID to Parse. I also discussed how to show different view controllers based on whether the user's shipping address is complete or not.

Chapter 13

Pay with Apple Pay

As an iOS developer, you have probably heard of Apple Pay. Apple Pay lets iPhone users pay for purchases by using their iPhones. There are some great benefits in store for a developer to integrate Apple Pay in his or her app. For example, your customers don't need to enter a credit card number, expiration date, and CVC numbers; or in some cases, shipping address and billing address before making a purchase. All of this means a faster and more convenient checkout process. Another benefit is that it's supposed to be a much secure way to handling credit card charges. In this chapter, I will show how to implement the feature of Pay with Apple Pay and Stripe.

Overview of Apple Pay

As a matter of fact, Apple Pay only handles part of the whole charge process. Namely, Apple Pay has completed the following things:

1. Authenticated a user, the iPhone owner, or a credit card holder.

2. Used a user interface to show what he or she is buying.

3. Provided you, the developer, with the shipping and billing addresses of the user.

4. Provided you, the developer, with a token so you can exchange it with a real payment processor, such as Stripe.

> **Note** To understand more about how Apple Pay works, please refer to
> https://developer.apple.com/apple-pay/Getting-Started-with-Apple-Pay.pdf.

Apple Pay and Stripe

> **Note**   In order to use Apple Pay, you'll need to add the "Apple Pay" capability to your app in Xcode. This requires creating, first, a merchant ID with Apple. You can read more about that process from the tutorial `https://stripe.com/docs/mobile/apple-pay`.

In Chapter 12, I have shown how to add Stripe/ApplePay CocoaPod to your project. After you have the merchant ID and "Apple Pay" capability set up, you can take full advantage of what the Stripe Apple Pay SDK has to offer. These are the steps:

1. Generate a PKPaymentRequest to submit to Apple.

2. Set the `paymentSummaryItems` property to an NSArray of PKPaymentSummaryItems. These are analogous to line items on a receipt and are used to explain our charges to the user.

3. After creating the request, query the device to see if Apple Pay is available (i.e., whether the app is running on the latest hardware and the user has added a valid credit card).

4. Create and display the payment request view controller.

5. After the payment request controller has returned a PKPayment, you can turn it into a single-use Stripe token with a simple method call.

6. Once you receive the Stripe token, call the Parse Cloud Function to make a real charge. The real charge will be handled by our back end, as we have done with Pay with Credit Card.

As you can see, the difference between Pay with Credit Card and Pay with Apple Pay is that you don't need to create an EMABPayment instance and save it while dealing with Pay with Apple Pay—Apple Pay on a user's device has the credit card information stored. Another benefit is that you don't need to ask for the user's shipping address; you can get it from the payment request.

Here is how to implement it, assuming you have registered a merchant ID through Apple Developer portal.

Write down your merchant ID with our EMABConstants class and name it kAppleMerchantID. Next, create a property to keep track of the PKPaymentRequest.

```
@property (nonatomic, strong) PKPaymentRequest *paymentRequest;
```

As mentioned before, you will need to use Apple's PKPaymentAuthorizationViewController. This view controller has some delegate methods you need to implement, so declare it:

```
@interface EMABBagTableViewController()<PKPaymentAuthorizationViewControllerDelegate>
```

Also, in order to show the items the user is purchasing, you need to set up the item list confirming PKPaymentAuthorizationViewController API PKPaymentSummaryItem. In other words, you need to transfer our EMABOrderItem to PKPaymentSummaryItem. Here is the helper method for that:

```
- (NSArray *)summaryItemsForShippingMethod:(PKShippingMethod *)shippingMethod {
    NSMutableArray *purchasedItems = [NSMutableArray arrayWithCapacity:[self.order.items
count]];
    for (EMABOrderItem *item in self.order.items) {
        double total = item.quantity * item.product.unitPrice;
        NSString *readable = [NSString stringWithFormat:@"%.2f",total];
        NSDecimalNumber *price = [NSDecimalNumber decimalNumberWithString:readable];
        PKPaymentSummaryItem *purchasedItem = [PKPaymentSummaryItem
summaryItemWithLabel:item.product.name amount:price];
        [purchasedItems addObject:purchasedItem];
    }

    return [NSArray arrayWithArray:purchasedItems];
}
```

Basically, you create a mutable array, iterate EMABOrderItem, and instantiate PKPaymentSummaryItem based on an instance of EMABOrderItem. In the end, you return an immutable copy of the container array.

Take a close look at the following two lines of code:

```
NSString *readable = [NSString stringWithFormat:@"%.2f",total];
NSDecimalNumber *price = [NSDecimalNumber decimalNumberWithString:readable];
```

This is definitely not the best way to represent the currency amount because normally you only have a two-digit mantissa for the currency amount. The recommended way by Apple Pay API is this:

```
NSDecimalNumber *price = [NSDecimalNumber decimalNumberWithMantissa:total exponent:-2
isNegative:NO];
```

Before you can initialize PKPaymentRequest, you need to know whether the user's iPhone is configured to Pay with Apple Pay. Luckily, Stripe has a convenient method for you: -(BOOL) canSubmitPaymentRequest. If yes, proceed ahead. If no, you need to gracefully report it to the user.

You also need to have the user's shipping address so you can mail the package. PKPaymentRequest has a method and setRequiredShippingAddressFields:PKAddressFieldPo stalAddress for that.

Here is the code:

```
-(IBAction)onApplePay:(id)sender{
    NSString *merchantId = kAppleMerchantID;
    self.paymentRequest = [Stripe paymentRequestWithMerchantIdentifier:merchantId];
    if ([Stripe canSubmitPaymentRequest:self.paymentRequest]) {
        [self.paymentRequest setRequiredShippingAddressFields:PKAddressFieldPostalAddress];
        [self.paymentRequest setRequiredBillingAddressFields:PKAddressFieldPostalAddress];
        self.paymentRequest.paymentSummaryItems = [self summaryItemsForShippingMethod:nil];
        PKPaymentAuthorizationViewController *auth = [[PKPaymentAuthorizationViewController
        alloc] initWithPaymentRequest:self.paymentRequest];
        auth.delegate = self;
        if (auth) {
            [self presentViewController:auth animated:YES completion:nil];
        } else
            [SVProgressHUD showErrorWithStatus:NSLocalizedString(@"Something Wrong",
            @"Something Wrong")];
    } else {
        [SVProgressHUD showErrorWithStatus:NSLocalizedString(@"Apple Pay is not enabled.
        Please enable your Apple Pay or Pay with Credit Card.", @"")];
    }

}
```

Next, present the PKPaymentAuthorizationViewController. The user taps to pay. What happens after the tap? Here's how to implement the view controller's delegate method:

```
-(void)paymentAuthorizationViewController:(nonnull PKPaymentAuthorizationViewController *)
controller didAuthorizePayment:(nonnull PKPayment *)payment completion:(nonnull void (^)
(PKPaymentAuthorizationStatus))completion{
    [self handlePaymentAuthorizationWithPayment:payment completion:nil];

}
```

Create the helper method handlePaymentAuthorizationWithPayment, then implement this method in "Creating a single-use token." Note that you have also been given a block that takes a PKPaymentAuthorizationStatus. Call this function with either PKPaymentAuthorizationStatusSuccess or PKPaymentAuthorizationStatusFailure after all of your asynchronous code is finished executing. This is how the PKPaymentAuthorizationViewController knows when and how to update its UI.

```
- (void)handlePaymentAuthorizationWithPayment:(PKPayment *)payment completion:(void (^)
(PKPaymentAuthorizationStatus))completion {

    [[STPAPIClient sharedClient] createTokenWithPayment:payment
                        completion:^(STPToken *token, NSError *error) {
                            if (error) {
                                completion(PKPaymentAuthorizationStatusFailure);
                                return;
                            }
```

```
                              [self createBackendChargeWithToken:token
                              completion:completion];
                    }];

}
```

Once you receive the charge token, call the Parse Cloud function to make a real charge:

```
- (void)createBackendChargeWithToken:(STPToken *)token
                        completion:(void (^)(PKPaymentAuthorizationStatus))completion {
    [self chargeWithToken:token.tokenId];
}
```

Here is how to call the Cloud function:

```
-(void)chargeWithToken:(NSString *)tokenId{
    [self.order saveInBackgroundWithBlock:^(BOOL success, NSError *error){
        if (!error) {
            __weak typeof(self) weakSelf = self;
            NSDictionary *params = @{@"chargeToken":tokenId, @"orderId":weakSelf.order.
objectId};
            [PFCloud callFunctionInBackground:@"ChargeToken" withParameters:params
block:^(NSString *message, NSError *error){
                if (!error) {
                    [weakSelf queryForUnfinishedOrder];
                }
            }];
        }
    }];
}
```

By all means, you want to save the current order first. After the save action is finished, pass the Stripe token and the order ID to the back end. It's a much safer practice. Once the charge is successfully run through, you make another API call to check whether the order status has been changed; also update your UI.

Summary

In this chapter, I briefly summarized how Apply Pay works and how you can implement the Pay with Apple Pay feature with Stripe's Apple Pay library.

14

Charge and E-Mail

In Chapter 12, I showed you how to use the cloud function to create and charge a Stripe Customer. In Chapter 13, I showed you how to use a cloud function to pay with Apple Pay. All three methods call functions of "createStripeCustomer," "chargeCustomer," and "chargeToken," respectively, in a JavaScript file with a name of "main.js" that you have written and hosted on Parse. The three functions take a dictionary input to execute and return either a string if successful or an NSError object if any error occurs. In this chapter, I will show you how you can implement these three JavaScript functions. In addition, you will learn how to use Mailgun to send an order confirmation once Stripe has successfully charged a user's credit card.

Create and Charge a Customer

To recap, here are the three JavaScript functions you will use in this chapter:

Create customer

```
[PFCloud callFunctionInBackground:@"createStripeCustomer" withParameters:stripeCustomerDicti
onary block:^(NSString *customerId, NSError *error) {
}];
```

Charge customer

```
[PFCloud callFunctionInBackground:@" chargeCustomer" withParameters:params block:^(NSString
*message, NSError *error){

}];
```

Pay with Apple Pay

```
[PFCloud callFunctionInBackground:@"ChargeToken" withParameters:params block:^(NSString
*message, NSError *error){
}];
```

Parse Cloud Code

First, here is some background on Parse Cloud Code. Parse Cloud Code is written in JavaScript and runs in the Parse Cloud rather than running on a mobile device. The Parse Cloud Code you write will work like your own back-end code. Obviously when your Cloud Code is updated, it becomes available to all mobile environments instantly. You don't have to wait for a new release of your application. This lets you change app behavior on the fly and adds new features faster. Figure 14-1 shows what your cloud function main.js looks like in Parse.

```
main.js
Parse.Cloud.define("createStripeCustomer",function(request,response){
    Parse.Cloud.useMasterKey();

    Parse.Promise.as().then(function(){
        return Stripe.Customers.create({
        description: 'Customer for        /',
        card:request.params.token,
        email:request.params.email

    }).then(null, function(error){
        console.log('Creating customer with stripe failed. Error: ' + error);
        return Parse.Promise.error('An error has occurred.');
    });

    }).then(function(customer) {
    response.success(customer.id);
}, function(error) {
    response.error(error);
    });
});
```

Figure 14-1. Cloud Code in Parse

The Parse Command-Line Tool (CLT)

Before you can use the Parse Cloud Code, you will need to install the Parse command-line tool on the computer you use for development. The command-line tool will help you deploy your code to the Parse Cloud. To install this tool, simply run the following command in the terminal:

```
curl -s https://www.parse.com/downloads/cloud_code/installer.sh | sudo /bin/bash
```

Once you have Parse CLT installed, you can start to set up a Cloud Code directory. Open the Terminal App, dir, to a directory where you want to put your Cloud Code directory, then type:

```
>parse configure accountKey -d
```

The CLT will response with:

```
> Input your account key or press enter to generate a new one.
Account Key: ${YOUR_ACCOUNT_KEY}
```

Press Enter, type the following command, and then press Enter again:

```
> parse new
```

The CLT will response with:

```
Would you like to create a new app, or add Cloud Code to an existing app?
Type "(n)ew" or "(e)xisting": e
1:  MyApp
2:  MyOtherApp
Select an App to add to config: 1
Awesome! Now it's time to setup some Cloud Code for the app: "MyApp",
Next we will create a directory to hold your Cloud Code.
Please enter the name to use for this directory,
or hit ENTER to use "MyApp" as the directory name.
```

Make your choice. Then enter:

```
> parse deploy
```

Once you have received a successful message from CLT, you can move to Parse.com, and look at the Cloud Code part in your project dashboard, as shown in Figure 14-1. You will see a simple "Hello World" cloud function.

From now on, you can work on the main.js in your local directory. Once you are ready to deploy, use:

```
> parse deploy
```

to deploy to the Parse server.

In the meantime, you can also read any log generated by Cloud Code or every time you make a Cloud Code function call, by tapping the "Logs" on Parse Dashboard, as shown in Figure 14-2.

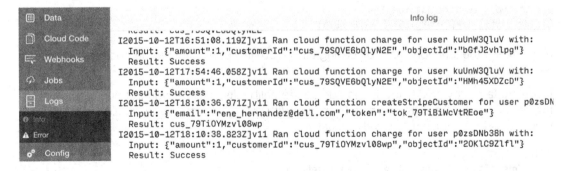

Figure 14-2. Cloud Code logs

> **Note**   To read more about the Parse Command-Line Tool, please visit `https://parse.com/` `apps/quickstart#cloud_code/unix`.

Parse Cloud Modules

To make developers' lives easier, Parse also provides the integration with third-party services and libraries through Cloud Modules. The Cloud Modules work just like JavaScript libraries. For this example, you will use Stripe Cloud Module and Mailgun Cloud Module.

```
/* Initialize the Stripe and Mailgun Cloud Modules */
var Stripe = require('stripe');
Stripe.initialize('YOUR_STRIPE_TEST_SECRET');

var Mailgun = require('mailgun');
Mailgun.initialize("YOUR_MAILGUN_PROJECT_NAME", "YOUR_MAILGUN_API_KEY");
```

Create a Stripe Customer

In Chapter 12, you learned how to use the "createStripeCustomer" cloud function to create a Stripe Customer. If you do use this method in your code, you will receive an error that states there is no function named "createStripeCustomer." So the first cloud function you will implement is "createStripeCustomer."

```
[PFCloud callFunctionInBackground:@"createStripeCustomer" withParameters:stripeCustomerDictionary
block:^(NSString *customerId, NSError *error) {
}];
```

First, you will need to include Stripe Cloud Module in your code; also specify the test secret key, as shown here:

```
var Stripe = require('stripe');
Stripe.initialize('YOUR_TEST_STRIPE_KEY);
```

Next, define the function name by calling `Parse.Cloud.define`. Just remember each function requires a unique name.

If you are familiar with JavaScript, in addition to callbacks, every asynchronous method in the Parse JavaScript SDK returns a Promise. With promises, your code can be much cleaner than the nested code you get with callbacks.

> **Note**   To read more about Parse Promise, refer to
> `https://parse.com/docs/js/guide` – promises.

Take a close look at the following simple Stripe Customer creation function:

```
Parse.Cloud.define("createStripeCustomer",function(request,response){
  Parse.Cloud.useMasterKey();

  Parse.Promise.as().then(function(){
    return Stripe.Customers.create({
    description: 'customer for Beauty & Me',
    card:request.params.tokenId,
        email:request.params.customerEmail

  }).then(null, function(error){
    console.log('Creating customer with stripe failed. Error: ' + error);
    return Parse.Promise.error('An error has occurred.');
  });
  }).then(function(customer) {
    response.success(customer.id);
  }, function(error) {
    response.error(error);
  });
});
```

Basically, you call the `Stripe.Customer.create` API to create a Stripe Customer. You provide the token you received from the iOS app and the user's e-mail to create the customer. If the customer is created successfully, you will receive the Stripe Customer object. Since you only need the customer id, return the id in the success response. You also let your iOS app know if there is any error.

Charge Customer

The next cloud function is "charge." What you received for this function is an order object id and a customer id. Here are the steps you need to follow:

1. Based on the order object id, find the order; you also need to include the products associated with the order and the customer. You will need this information to generate a receipt.

2. Charge the customer based on the Stripe Customer id.

3. Update the order with a new ORDER_COMPLETED status, and then generate a real order id and a big integer number, based on the total orders we have in the system.

4. Send an e-mail to the customer by calling Mailgun Parse Cloud Module. You might have to compose some e-mail content by mixing html tag and the order's information.

5. Once the order confirmation e-mail is sent successfully, send a message back to the iOS app. If any errors occur, return the errors.

Here is the code for the previous five steps:

```
/* Initialize the Stripe and Mailgun Cloud Modules */
var Stripe = require('stripe');
Stripe.initialize('your_own_stripe_secret);
var Mailgun = require('mailgun');
Mailgun.initialize("your_mailgun_email_account", "your_mailgun_key");

Parse.Cloud.define("chargeCustomer", function(request, response) {
  Parse.Cloud.useMasterKey();
  var order;
  var orderNo;
  Parse.Promise.as().then(function() {
    var orderQuery = new Parse.Query('Order');
    orderQuery.equalTo('objectId', request.params.orderId);
    orderQuery.include("customer");

    orderQuery.include(["items.product"]);
    orderQuery.descending("createdAt");

    return orderQuery.first().then(null, function(error) {
      return Parse.Promise.error('Sorry, this order doesn\'t exist.');
    });

  }).then(function(result) {
    order = result;
  }).then(function(result) {
    var countQuery = new Parse.Query("Order");
    return countQuery.count().then(null,function(error){
        return Parse.Promise.error('Something wrong.');
    });
  }).then(function(result) {
    orderNo = result;
  }).then(function(order){
    eturn Stripe.Charges.create({
    amount: request.params.amount, // express dollars in cents
    currency: "usd",
    customer:request.params.customerId
    }).then(null, function(error) {
      console.log('Charging with stripe failed. Error: ' + error);
      return Parse.Promise.error('An error has occurred. Your credit card was not
      charged.');
    });
  }).then(function(purchase) {
    orderNo = 1000000+orderNo;
    order.set('stripePaymentId', purchase.id);
    order.set('orderStatus', 1);  // order made
    order.set('orderNo', orderNo);
    return order.save().then(null, function(error) {
      return Parse.Promise.error('A critical error has occurred with your order. Please ' +
                            'contact info@beauty4you.co at your earliest convinience. ');
    });
```

```
}). then(function(result) {
  var greeting = "Dear ";
  if (request.params.name !== "N/A")
    greeting +=  request.params.name + ",\n\n";
  else
    greeting += request.params.email + ",\n\n";
  var orderId = "Order No. " + orderNo + "\n";
  var body = greeting + orderId + "  We have received your order for the following
  item(s): \n\n" +
          request.params.itemDesc + "\n";

              var note = "Note: " + request.params.note +"\n\n";
  body += "\Total: $" +  (request.params.amount / 100.00).toFixed(2) + "\n\n" + note;

  var thankyou = "Contact us if you have any question!\n\n" +
  "\n Thank you,\n" + "Beauty 4 You Team";

  body += thankyou;

  // Send the email.
  return Mailgun.sendEmail({
    to: request.params.email,
    bcc: 'CUSTOMER-EMAIL',
    from: 'YOUR-EMAIL',
    subject: '',
    text: body
  }).then(null, function(error) {
    return Parse.Promise.error('Your purchase was successful, but we were not able to ' +
                          'send you an email. Contact us at YOUR-EMAIL ' +
                          'you have any questions.');
  });

}).then(function() {
  // And we're done!
  response.success('Success');
}, function(error) {
  response.error(error);
});
});
```

Charge Token

This function is almost identical to the "chargeCustomer" function. The only difference is that you need to use a card property in the Stripe.Charges.create function:

```
Stripe.Charges.create({
  amount: request.params.amount, // express dollars in cents
  currency: "usd",
  card:request.params.customerId})
```

Summary

In this chapter, I showed you how to create a Stripe Customer ID and then use this customer ID to charge a user's credit card from Parse Cloud Module. I also explained how to use Mailgun to send an order confirmation e-mail to this user.

Chapter 15

My Account

At this point, the app can finish its main job—buy and then pay for products. However, there is still some work to do to make it a complete app. For instance, users should be able to change their shipping addresses and update their payment methods. They should also be able to look up the products they marked as favorites, look up their order history, and log out of their account—none of these features have been implemented yet.

In this chapter you will learn how to:

- Implement a static "My Account" screen. This screen is where a user can sign out or log in, depending on whether you have a logged-in user; show one's shipping address; visit order history; and manage payment methods.

- Allow a user to visit and edit one's shipping address.

- Let the user visit one's order history.

- Let a user manage one's payment methods.

- Enable a user to manage one's favorite list.

Create the My Account Screen

Start by creating a UITableViewController subclass and name it EMABUserAccountTableViewController. Next, you will organize some static information into the UITableView. Define an enum type for the cell content you need.

```
typedef NS_OPTIONS(NSInteger, TABLE_ROW){
    SIGNED_IN = 0,
    CONTACT_INFO = 1,
    PAYMENT = 2,
    FAVORITE = 3,
    HISTORY
};
```

You also need a property to represent the current logged-in user.

```
@interface EMABUserAccountTableViewController ()
@property (nonatomic, strong) EMABUser *customer;
@end
```

In general, this screen is pretty simple to implement. Most of the following code is self-explanatory:

```
@implementation EMABUserAccountTableViewController

- (void)viewDidLoad {
    [super viewDidLoad];
    self.customer = [EMABUser currentUser];
}
```

The user is instantiated on -(void)viewDidLoad. If there is no logged-in user, self. customer will be nil. You will use this information to decide how many cells you need for the UITableView.

```
#pragma mark - Table view data source

- (NSInteger)numberOfSectionsInTableView:(UITableView *)tableView {
    // Return the number of sections.
    return 1;
}

- (NSInteger)tableView:(UITableView *)tableView numberOfRowsInSection:(NSInteger)section {
    // Return the number of rows in the section.
    return (self.customer)?5:1;
}
```

If there is no valid user, only one cell is returned; for any valid user, five cells are created.

```
- (UITableViewCell *)tableView:(UITableView *)tableView cellForRowAtIndexPath:(NSIndexPath
*)indexPath {
    UITableViewCell *cell = [tableView dequeueReusableCellWithIdentifier:@"AccountCell"
forIndexPath:indexPath];

    // Configure the cell…
    NSString *title = @"";
    NSString *subtitle = @"";
    switch (indexPath.row) {
        case SIGNED_IN:
            title = (self.customer)?NSLocalizedString(@"Sign In", @""):
NSLocalizedString(@"Sign Out", @"");
            subtitle = self.customer.email;
            break;
        case CONTACT_INFO:
            title = NSLocalizedString(@"Contact Info", @"");
            break;
```

```
        case PAYMENT:
            title = NSLocalizedString(@"Payment", @"");
            break;
        case FAVORITE:
            title = NSLocalizedString(@"Favorite", @"");
            break;
        case HISTORY:
            title = NSLocalizedString(@"Order History", @"");
            break;

        default:
            break;
    }
    cell.textLabel.text = title;
    cell.detailTextLabel.text = subtitle;
    return cell;
}
```

The following UITableView delegate methods accomplish two things:

- The first cell is for letting users sign out if the cell is tapped, corresponding to "Sign Out" text. For a user not logged in, the Signup or Login screen is displayed, corresponding to "Log In" text.

- The remaining cells present the different view controllers based on the cell selected.

```
#pragma mark -
-(void)tableView:(UITableView *)tableView didSelectRowAtIndexPath:(NSIndexPath *)indexPath  {
    NSString *viewControllerIdentifier = @"";
    switch (indexPath.row) {
        case SIGNED_IN:
            if (self.customer) {
                [self signOut];
            } else {
                [self presentSignupOrLogin];
            }
            break;
        case CONTACT_INFO:
            viewControllerIdentifier = @"EMABUserProfileTableViewController";
            break;
        case FAVORITE:
            viewControllerIdentifier = @"MABUserFavoriteHistoryTableViewControlle";
            break;
        case HISTORY:
            viewControllerIdentifier = @"EMABUserOrderHistoryTableViewController";
            break;
        case PAYMENT:
            viewControllerIdentifier = @"EMABUserPaymentMethodTableViewController";
            break;
        default:
            break;
    }
```

```
    if ([viewControllerIdentifier length] > 0) {
        UIViewController *viewController = [self.storyboard
instantiateViewControllerWithIdentifier:viewControllerIdentifier];
        [self.navigationController pushViewController:viewController animated:YES];
    }

}

-(void)signOut {
    [EMABUser logOut];
    [self.tableView reloadData];
}

-(void)presentSignupOrLogin {
    UIStoryboard *dispatchStoryboard = [UIStoryboard storyboardWithName:@"LoginSignup"
bundle:nil];
    UINavigationController *navController = (UINavigationController *)[dispatchStoryboard
instantiateInitialViewController];
    [self presentViewController:navController animated:YES completion:nil];
}
@end
```

Figure 15-1 shows the final result.

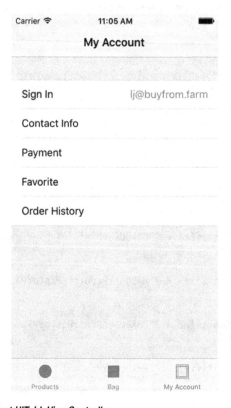

Figure 15-1. Screen of My Account UITableViewController

Contact Info

I have shown you how to implement EMABUserProfileTableViewController in Chapter 11. When a user wants to view and edit his or her shipping address, he or she has a chance to open EMABUserProfileTableViewController from "Contact Info" in "My Account," then view and edit if necessary.

Payment Method

Customers may use different credit cards, whether they shop at a brick and mortar store, online, or via an app. If you save an EMABPaymentMethod instance every time you see a different credit card, the user might have several cards stored with you. You need to provide a place for the user to manage those credit cards, such as setting one card as the default one, deleting a credit card, or adding a new one.

This section covers how to display all credit cards associated with a user, as well as how to let users add additional ones and/or delete some.

The model for this section is the EMABPaymentMethod model.

View

Use a standard UITableViewCell to display the basic credit card information such as the card's last four digits and expiration date. Figure 15-2 shows the basic UITableViewCell.

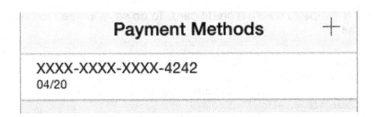

Figure 15-2. The Payment method cell shows the last four digits and the expiration date

Controller

For the controller, create a PFQueryTableViewController subclass and name it EMABUserPaymentMethodTableViewController. Here is how to use PFQueryTableViewController, covered in the previous chapter:

```
- (void)awakeFromNib {
    [super awakeFromNib];
    self.parseClassName = kPaymentMethod;
    self.objectsPerPage = 10;
    self.paginationEnabled = YES;
    self.pullToRefreshEnabled = YES;
}
```

```
- (PFQuery *)queryForTable {
    PFQuery *query = [EMABPaymentMethod queryForOwner:[EMABUser currentUser]];
    if ([self.objects count] == 0) {
        query.cachePolicy = kPFCachePolicyCacheThenNetwork;
    }
    return query;
}
```

The EMABPaymentMethod model uses a helper query method, +(PFQuery
*)queryForOwner:(EMABUser *)user;

```
#pragma mark - UITableView Datasource
- (UITableViewCell *)tableView:(UITableView *)tableView cellForRowAtIndexPath:(NSIndexPath
*)indexPath object:(EMABPaymentMethod *)object{
    UITableViewCell *cell = [tableView dequeueReusableCellWithIdentifier:@"PaymentMethodCell"
forIndexPath:indexPath];
    if (indexPath.row == [[self objects] count]) {
        cell.textLabel.text = NSLocalizedString(@"Load More…", @"");
    } else {
        cell.textLabel.text = [object friendlyCreditCardNumber];
        cell.detailTextLabel.text = [object friendlyExpirationMonthYear];
    }
    return cell;
}
```

For each cell, use the EMABPaymentMethod helper method to show two pieces of
information: a formatted last four digits and the expiration date.

You want the user to swipe to delete a credit card. To do so, you need to declare this with
-(void)viewDidLoad.

```
UISwipeGestureRecognizer *leftSwipe = [[UISwipeGestureRecognizer alloc] initWithTarget:self
action:@selector(onLeftSwipe:)];
        [leftSwipe setDirection:UISwipeGestureRecognizerDirectionRight];
        leftSwipe.delegate = self;
        [self.tableView addGestureRecognizer:leftSwipe];
```

When a user makes a left swipe gesture, you find out which cell is swept based on the point
on the screen. Then call the PFObject asynchronous deletion method, and make another
query method call to update the UI:

```
-(void)onLeftSwipe:(UIGestureRecognizer *)gestureRecognizer
{
    CGPoint point = [gestureRecognizer locationInView:self.tableView];
    NSIndexPath *indexPath = [self.tableView indexPathForRowAtPoint:point];
    if (indexPath) {
        EMABPaymentMethod *paymentMethod = (EMABPaymentMethod *)[self
objectAtIndexPath:indexPath];
        __weak typeof(self) weakSelf = self;
        [paymentMethod deleteInBackgroundWithBlock:^(BOOL succeeded, NSError *error) {
```

```
            if (!error) {
                [weakSelf loadObjects];
            }
        }];
    }
}
```

As shown in Figure 15-3, the "+" bar button item (see Chapter 2) is set up to allow the user to add a new credit card. You have had EMABAddCreditCardViewController, so simply present it; a EMABPayment instance will be created in the process.

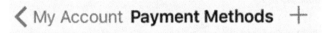

Figure 15-3. *A "+" bar button item on UINavigationBar lets users add another payment method*

Here is the code:

```
#pragma mark - IBAction
-(IBAction)onAdd:(id)sender
{
    EMABAddCreditCardViewController *viewController =
(EMABAddCreditCardViewController *)[self.storyboard
instantiateViewControllerWithIdentifier:@"EMABAddCreditCardViewController"];
        __weak typeof(self) weakSelf = self;
        viewController.finishBlock = ^(NSString *customerId){
            [weakSelf loadObjects];
        };
        [self.navigationController pushViewController:viewController animated:YES];

}

@end
```

In the previous code, -(void)loadObjects is a PFQueryTableViewController method. You use it to make an API request to load new credit card information and show it on this table view.

My Order History

Per requirements, users should be able to browse all of their order history and also view details for a particular order. In this section, I cover how to implement this feature.

View

Figure 15-4 shows how you want to display a user's order history in a UITableViewCell. It's pretty simple. Use, in this order, a UILabel to show the order date, a UILabel to show the total amount of the order, and the product's name. You might have multiple products in one order. Since you don't have the space for displaying all products in an order, only show the first one.

You can use a helper method to connect your data model with this view:

```
-(void)configureItem:(EMABOrder *)item;
```

Figure 15-4. *A basic order history cell*

```
#import "PFTableViewCell.h"

@class EMABOrder;
@interface EMABOrderHistoryTableViewCell : PFTableViewCell

-(void)configureItem:(EMABOrder *)item;
@end
```

Here is the implementation file:

```
#import "EMABOrderHistoryTableViewCell.h"
#import "EMABOrder.h"

@interface EMABOrderHistoryTableViewCell()
@property (nonatomic, weak) IBOutlet UILabel *dateLabel;
@property (nonatomic, weak) IBOutlet UILabel *totalLabel;
@property (nonatomic, weak) IBOutlet UILabel *nameLabel;
@end

@implementation EMABOrderHistoryTableViewCell

-(void)configureItem:(EMABOrder *)item
{
    if (item) {
        NSDateFormatter *dateFormatter = [[NSDateFormatter alloc] init];
        [dateFormatter setDateStyle:NSDateFormatterMediumStyle];
        [dateFormatter setTimeStyle:NSDateFormatterMediumStyle];

        self.dateLabel.text = [dateFormatter stringFromDate:item.updatedAt];
        self.totalLabel.text = [item friendlyTotal];
        self.nameLabel.text = [item.items[0] name];
    }
}

@end
```

Controller

Create a PFQueryTableViewController subclass, and name it
EMABUserOrderHistoryViewController. For this view controller, the whole implementation is
straightforward.

```
@implementation EMABUserOrderHistoryViewController

- (void)awakeFromNib {
    [super awakeFromNib];
    self.parseClassName = kOrder;
    self.objectsPerPage = 10;
    self.paginationEnabled = YES;
    self.pullToRefreshEnabled = YES;
}

- (void)viewDidLoad {
    [super viewDidLoad];
    // Do any additional setup after loading the view.
    self.title = NSLocalizedString(@"Order History", @"Order History");
}

- (void)didReceiveMemoryWarning {
    [super didReceiveMemoryWarning];
    // Dispose of any resources that can be recreated.
}

- (PFQuery *)queryForTable {
    PFQuery *query = [EMABOrder queryForCustomer:[EMABUser currentUser] orderStatus:ORDER_
MADE];
    if ([self.objects count] == 0) {
        query.cachePolicy = kPFCachePolicyCacheThenNetwork;
    }
    return query;
}

-(CGFloat)tableView:(UITableView *)tableView heightForRowAtIndexPath:(NSIndexPath *)
indexPath
{
    return 60.0;
}
- (EMABOrderHistoryTableViewCell *)tableView:(UITableView *)tableView cellForRowAtIndexPath:
(NSIndexPath *)indexPath object:(EMABOrder *)object{
    EMABOrderHistoryTableViewCell *cell = [tableView dequeueReusableCellWithIdentifier:
@"HistoryCell" forIndexPath:indexPath];
    [cell configureItem:object];
    return cell;
}
```

```
#pragma mark - Navigation

// In a storyboard-based application, you will often want to do a little preparation before
navigation
- (void)prepareForSegue:(UIStoryboardSegue *)segue sender:(id)sender {
    // Get the new view controller using [segue destinationViewController].
    // Pass the selected object to the new view controller.
    if ([segue.identifier isEqualToString:@"ShowOrderDetail"]){
        NSIndexPath *indexPath = [self.tableView indexPathForSelectedRow];

        EMABOrder *order = self.objects[indexPath.row];
        EMABOrderDetailTableViewController *viewController = segue.
destinationViewController;
        [viewController setOrder:order];
    }
}
}

@end
```

When a user taps an order cell, more information about the order is displayed. This order detail screen might be very close to the EMABBagTableViewController. However, you won't let the user change the order items, and there are no payment options, obviously. This can be achieved in one of two ways: you can reuse EMABBagTableViewController and hide the UI controls you don't want to show, or you create another view controller. For this example, use the second approach. One reason is that the EMABBagTableViewController has already been quite messy. The other is that you might want to add more features later. It's easier when you don't have that much code to mess around with.

Start by creating a new UITableViewController, and name it EMABOrderDetailTableViewController. You still want to show the order number, order date, complete description, and total amount of an order. In the same fashion, use a UITableView header view to show the order number and the order date; use UITableView footer view to show the complete description and the total amount.

For each UITableViewCell, show each item's name, unit price, and quantity. Here is the implementation:

```
#import "EMABOrderDetailTableViewController.h"
#import "EMABOrder.h"
#import "EMABOrderItem.h"
#import "EMABProduct.h"
@interface EMABOrderDetailTableViewController ()
@property (nonatomic, weak) IBOutlet UILabel *ordeNoLabel;
@property (nonatomic, weak) IBOutlet UILabel *ordeDateLabel;
@property (nonatomic, weak) IBOutlet UILabel *totalLabel;
@property (nonatomic, weak) IBOutlet UILabel *totalTextLabel;
@end
```

```objc
@implementation EMABOrderDetailTableViewController

-(void)setOrder:(EMABOrder *)order
{
    if (_order != order) {
        _order = order;

        [self configureView];
    }

}

-(void)configureView {
    self.ordeNoLabel.text = [self.order friendlyOrderNo];
    NSDateFormatter *dateFormatter = [[NSDateFormatter alloc] init];
    [dateFormatter setDateStyle:NSDateFormatterMediumStyle];
    [dateFormatter setTimeStyle:NSDateFormatterShortStyle];
    self.ordeDateLabel.text = [dateFormatter stringFromDate:[NSDate date]];
    self.totalLabel.text = [self.order friendlyTotal];

    [self.tableView reloadData];
}

- (void)viewDidLoad {
    [super viewDidLoad];
    self.title = NSLocalizedString(@"Order Detail", @"Order Detail");
    [self configureView];
}

- (void)didReceiveMemoryWarning {
    [super didReceiveMemoryWarning];
    // Dispose of any resources that can be recreated.
}

#pragma mark - Table view data source

- (NSInteger)numberOfSectionsInTableView:(UITableView *)tableView {
    // Return the number of sections.
    return 1;
}

- (NSInteger)tableView:(UITableView *)tableView numberOfRowsInSection:(NSInteger)section {
    // Return the number of rows in the section.
    return [self.order.items count];
}
```

```
- (UITableViewCell *)tableView:(UITableView *)tableView cellForRowAtIndexPath:
(NSIndexPath *)indexPath {
    UITableViewCell *cell = [tableView dequeueReusableCellWithIdentifier:@"OrderItemCell"
    forIndexPath:indexPath];

    if (self.order) {
        EMABOrderItem *item = self.order.items[indexPath.row];
        cell.textLabel.text = item.product.name;
        cell.detailTextLabel.text = [NSString stringWithFormat:@"%@ x %lld",
        [item.product friendlyPrice], item.quantity];
    }
    return cell;
}

@end
```

Favorite Products

This shows you how to display a user's list of favorite products, and it allows a user to remove a product from the list. You also enable the user to tap an item on this list to see the product detail.

Model

Use the EMABFavoriteProduct model introduced in Chapter 7.

View

Reuse the EMABProductTableViewCell, introduced in Chapter 6. See Figure 15-5.

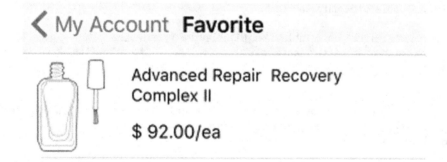

Figure 15-5. The Favorite product cell

Controller

Create a PFQueryTableViewController subclass, and name it
EMABUserFavoriteHistoryTableViewController.

```objc
#import "EMABUserFavoriteHistoryTableViewController.h"
#import "EMABConstants.h"
#import "EMABFavoriteProduct.h"
#import "EMABProduct.h"
#import "EMABUser.h"
#import "EMABProductTableViewCell.h"
#import "EMABProductDetailViewController.h"

@implementation EMABUserFavoriteHistoryTableViewController

- (void)awakeFromNib {
    [super awakeFromNib];
    self.parseClassName = kProduct;
    self.objectsPerPage = 10;
    self.paginationEnabled = YES;
    self.pullToRefreshEnabled = YES;
}

- (PFQuery *)queryForTable {
    PFQuery *query = [EMABFavoriteProduct queryForCustomer:[EMABUser currentUser]];
    if ([self.objects count] == 0) {
        query.cachePolicy = kPFCachePolicyCacheThenNetwork;
    }
    return query;
}

#pragma mark - UITableView Datasource

-(CGFloat)tableView:(UITableView *)tableView heightForRowAtIndexPath:(NSIndexPath *)
indexPath
{
    return 80.0;
}

- (EMABProductTableViewCell *)tableView:(UITableView *)tableView cellForRowAtIndexPath:
(NSIndexPath *)indexPath object:(EMABFavoriteProduct *)object{
    EMABProductTableViewCell *cell = [tableView dequeueReusableCellWithIdentifier:@"Product
Cell" forIndexPath:indexPath];
    if (indexPath.row == [[self objects] count]) {
        cell.textLabel.text = NSLocalizedString(@"Load More…", @"");
    } else {
        [cell configureItem:object.product];
    }
    return cell;
}
```

To make this list editable, use the UITableView delegate method, tableView: (UITableView *)tableView commitEditingStyle:(UITableViewCellEditingStyle) editingStyle forRowAtIndexPath:(NSIndexPath *)indexPath.

First, give the user a button so you know the user has the intention to edit. Add a bar button item as the right-bar button item of UINavigationItem, and use the system Edit button style.

Second, enable the row's "editing mode" by calling the following method:

```
-(BOOL)tableView:(UITableView *)tableView canEditRowAtIndexPath:(NSIndexPath *)indexPath{
    return YES;
}
```

Once a user taps the "Edit" button, a red "-" appears on each cell. Tap the "-" icon, and the following method will be executed:

```
-(void)tableView:(UITableView *)tableView commitEditingStyle:(UITableViewCellEditingStyle)
editingStyle forRowAtIndexPath:(NSIndexPath *)indexPath
{
    if (editingStyle == UITableViewCellEditingStyleDelete) {
        EMABFavoriteProduct *fProduct = (EMABFavoriteProduct *)[self
objectAtIndexPath:indexPath];
        [fProduct deleteInBackgroundWithBlock:^(BOOL succeeded, NSError *error) {
            if (!error) {
                [self loadObjects];
            }
        }];
    }
}
```

You will only listen to the delete action and call the PFObject asynchronous deletion method. Once the deletion is finished successfully, query the back-end server and update the UI.

When a user taps a product on the list, the product detail is displayed. You have had EMABProductDetailViewController in place; you only need to pass the right EMABProduct instance to it. Since your PFQuery returns the list of EMABFavoriteProduct, you need to take an extra step to get the EMABProduct. Here is the code:

```
#pragma mark - UITableView Delegate
-(void)tableView:(UITableView *)tableView didSelectRowAtIndexPath:(NSIndexPath *)indexPath{
    if (indexPath.row == [[self objects] count]) {
        [self loadNextPage];
    } else {
        EMABProductDetailViewController *viewController = [self.storyboard
instantiateViewControllerWithIdentifier:@"EMABProductDetailViewController"];
        [viewController setProduct:(EMABProduct*)[self objectAtIndexPath:indexPath]];
        [self.navigationController pushViewController:viewController animated:YES];
    }
}

@end
```

Summary

In this chapter, I have shown you how to implement a basic "My Account" screen. Based on whether a user is logged in or not, we presented different content for each scenario. I also demonstrated how a logged-in user can see one's shipping address, payment methods, favorites list, and order history. On the other hand, I will only show "Sign In" when we don't have a signed-in user.

I also showed how to use PFQueryTableViewController to show a user's credit card information that has previously been entered. Then I showed you who to let the user add a new credit card or delete an existing one, and how to view a user's order history and a specific order's detail.

Finally, I discussed how to display a list of favotie products. Following this, you learned how to show the product detail while the user tapped one product on the list.

Chapter 16

Add Product

So far, you have added products for your app through the Parse project dashboard on Parse.com. Once your app goes live, it probably isn't a good idea to allow everyone to do this. A few issues might arise if you let everyone access the Parse Dashboard.

- You might expose too much information to people who are not supposed to know it.
- There is a chance that you will enter your data incorrectly.
- Your data could be easily deleted or altered.

In general, Parse Dashboard is neither a user-friendly interface nor an efficient way to manually enter a lot of data.

Typically you will create a web app to let some admin users add or edit products. Generally speaking, it's much more efficient to use a web app to do data entry work. For the completeness of this book, I will introduce you to how to create an admin user and provide a special interface for this user to add or edit products from the mobile app. Some use cases for this feature might include a small shop that doesn't have many products to enter or a business that needs to take a lot of product photos and upload them to the server.

Model

First, you need to add a new Boolean property to your EMABUser model and name it isAdmin;:

`@property (nonatomic, assign) BOOL isAdmin;`You also need to add it to the @dynamic list in the EMABUser implementation file.

By the time a user signs up with your app, as discussed in Chapter 8, you will update the user's isAdmin property to true in the Parse Dashboard.

View

Add a new section in EMABUserAccountTableViewController, as discussed in Chapter 15, to display some content only for an admin user.

```
-(NSInteger)numberOfSectionsInTableView:(UITableView *)tableView {
    // Return the number of sections.
    return (self.customer && self.customer.isAdmin)?2:1;
}
```

You only need one cell for this section. This cell will have a title "Add product." When the cell is tapped, you will present a product add screen. Figure 16-1 shows what the screen looks like. This screen has a PFImageView to show the thumbnail of this product. When an admin taps the image view, you will ask whether he or she wants to upload an image from the phone's camera roll or take a new photo. You also have a UITextField to let the admin write the product name and a UITextField to write the product's unit price and price unit. You have another UITextField for the product brand and, in the end, a UITextView for the product description.

Figure 16-1. Add a product screen

Here are some of the properties to represent all UI controls:

```
@property (nonatomic, weak) IBOutlet PFImageView *productImageView;
@property (nonatomic, weak) IBOutlet UITextField *nameTextField;
@property (nonatomic, weak) IBOutlet UITextField *priceTextField;
@property (nonatomic, weak) IBOutlet UITextField *unitTextField;
@property (nonatomic, weak) IBOutlet UITextField *brandTextField;
@property (nonatomic, weak) IBOutlet UITextView *desciptionTextView;
```

Controller

Create a new UIViewController subclass, and name it
"EMABAddProductTableViewController." Before you dive into the implementation, think
about what the view controller is supposed to do.

1. You will need to implement a feature to upload a product image
   to Parse.

2. You will let an admin enter a product's name, price, unit price, and
   product summary.

3. You will let an admin enter this product's brand. This will be a better
   user experience because you let this admin choose a brand from a list.

4. You need to make sure that all information is entered by this admin
   before one taps "Save."

5. When an admin starts to type something, a software keyboard will
   show up and occupy part of the screen. You need to handle this case
   so your admin can always see everything he or she is typing.

I will address these five tasks one by one.

Upload a Product Photo

Firstl, you can add a tap gesture on the product image view, as shown in the following
snippet:

```
-(void)setupProductImageview
{
    UITapGestureRecognizer *portraitTap = [[UITapGestureRecognizer alloc]
    initWithTarget:self action:@selector(onThumbnail:)];
    [self.productImageView addGestureRecognizer:portraitTap];
}
```

Once an admin taps the image view, you ask whether to upload a photo from the Camera Roll or take a new photo. This is implemented in the onThumbnail: method:

```
-(void)onThumbnail:(UITapGestureRecognizer *)recognizer{
        //ask to add new receipt
    UIAlertController* alert = [UIAlertController alertControllerWithTitle:
    NSLocalizedString(@"Photo Source", @"Photo Source")
                                    message:NSLocalizedString(@"Choose One", @"Choose One")
                                    preferredStyle:UIAlertControllerStyleActionSheet];
    UIAlertAction* cancelAction = [UIAlertAction actionWithTitle:@"Cancel" style:
                                    UIAlertActionStyleCancel
                                    handler:^(UIAlertAction * action) {
                                    }];

    UIAlertAction* photoLibraryAction = [UIAlertAction actionWithTitle:@"Photo Library"
                                        style:UIAlertActionStyleDefault
                                        handler:^(UIAlertAction * action) {
                                        [self showImagePickerForSourceType:
                                        UIImagePickerControllerSourceTypePhotoLibrary];
                                        }];
    UIAlertAction* cameraAction = [UIAlertAction actionWithTitle:@"Camera"
                                     style:UIAlertActionStyleDefault
                                     handler:^(UIAlertAction * action) {
                                     [self showImagePickerForSourceType:
                                     UIImagePickerController
                                     SourceTypeCamera];
                                     }];

    [alert addAction:cancelAction];
    [alert addAction:photoLibraryAction];
    [alert addAction:cameraAction];

    [self presentViewController:alert animated:YES completion:nil];

}
```

The following is the implementation of the image picker based on the source type. If the source type is UIImagePickerControllerSourceTypePhotoLibrary, you don't really need to do too much. The UIImagePickerController delegate method will send back with the image data selected. If the source type is UIImagePickerControllerSourceTypeCamera, it's a little bit complicated. First, you will need to add two bar button items. One is for "Cancel". The other is for "Take Photo". Second, you want to provide an overlay over the camera overview to let the admin crop the overlay area.

Here is the complete implementation:

```
- (void)showImagePickerForSourceType:(UIImagePickerControllerSourceType)sourceType
{
    imagePickerController = [[UIImagePickerController alloc] init];
    imagePickerController.modalPresentationStyle = UIModalPresentationCurrentContext;
    imagePickerController.sourceType = sourceType;
    imagePickerController.delegate = self;
```

```
    if (sourceType == UIImagePickerControllerSourceTypeCamera)
    {
        CGRect frame =  [UIScreen mainScreen].applicationFrame;
        UIToolbar *toolBar=[[UIToolbar alloc] initWithFrame:CGRectMake(0, frame.size.
        height-44, self.view.frame.size.width, 44)];

        toolBar.barStyle =  UIBarStyleBlackOpaque;
        NSArray *items=@[
                        [[UIBarButtonItem alloc] initWithBarButtonSystemItem:UIBarButtonSys
                        temItemCancel  target:self action:@selector(cancelPicture:)],
                        [[UIBarButtonItem alloc] initWithBarButtonSystemItem:UIBarButtonSys
                        temItemFlexibleSpace  target:nil action:nil],
                        [[UIBarButtonItem alloc] initWithBarButtonSystemItem:UIBarButtonSys
                        temItemCamera  target:self action:@selector(shootPicture:)]
                        ];
        [toolBar setItems:items];

        // create the overlay view
        UIView *overlayView = [[UIView alloc] initWithFrame:CGRectMake(0.0, 64.0,
        frame.size.width, frame.size.height-44.0)];
        overlayView.opaque=NO;
        overlayView.backgroundColor=[UIColor clearColor];

        // parent view for our overlay
        UIView *cameraView=[[UIView alloc] initWithFrame:frame];
        [cameraView addSubview:overlayView];
        [cameraView addSubview:toolBar];

        imagePickerController.showsCameraControls = NO;
        imagePickerController.extendedLayoutIncludesOpaqueBars = YES;
        [imagePickerController setCameraOverlayView:cameraView];
        EMABAppDelegate* appDel = (EMABAppDelegate*)[[UIApplication sharedApplication] delegate];
        [appDel.tabBarController presentViewController:imagePickerController animated:YES
        completion:^{

        }];
    } else
        [self.parentViewController presentViewController:imagePickerController animated:YES
        completion:nil];
}
```

It's pretty simple to implement the "Cancel" and "Take Photo" bar button item methods:

```
#pragma mark - ImagePickerController
-(IBAction)cancelPicture:(id)sender{
    [self dismissViewControllerAnimated:YES completion:nil];
}

-(IBAction)shootPicture:(id)sender{ shootPicture
    [imagePickerController takePicture];
}
```

In the end, you need to implement the delegate method of UIImagePickerController: -(void) imagePickerController: DidFinishPickingMediaWithInfo.

In this method, you will need to do two things. First, you crop the image to a smaller size—in this case, 408 pixels in width—and upload it as a thumbnail of the product image. Second, the image taken from Camera App is still too big so you scale it a little bit smaller, in this case, 1632 pixels in width. I chose 408 and 1632 based on the tradeoff between the speed to upload to the Parse server and the reasonable resolution of an image's quality.

The next step is to convert UIIamge to PFFile. You can use the PFFile class method, (PFFile *)fileWithName:(NSString *)filename data:(NSData *)data. Once you have PFFile instances for a full-size image and a thumbnail image, you need to save the two PFFile to Parse. When the save action is completed successfully, you need to assign the two PFFile to this product.

Here is the full implementation:

```
// This method is called when an image has been chosen from the library or taken from the camera.
- (void)imagePickerController:(UIImagePickerController *)picker
  didFinishPickingMediaWithInfo:(NSDictionary *)info
{
    UIImage *image = [info valueForKey:UIImagePickerControllerOriginalImage];
    UIImage *fullsize = [UIImage imageWithImage:image scaledToWidth:1632];
    UIImage *thumbnail = [UIImage imageWithImage:fullsize scaledToWidth:408];

    self.productImageView.image = image;

    __weak typeof(self) weakSelf = self;

    PFFile *fullsizeFile = [PFFile fileWithName:@"fullszie.jpg" data:UIImageJPEGRepresentati
    on(fullsize, 0.75)];

    [fullsizeFile saveInBackgroundWithBlock:^(BOOL success, NSError *error){
        if (!error) {
            weakSelf.product.fullsizeImage = fullsizeFile;
        }else {
            NSLog(@"error:%@",[error localizedDescription]);
        }
    }];
    PFFile *thumbnailFile = [PFFile fileWithName:@"thumbnail.jpg"
    data:UIImageJPEGRepresentation(thumbnail, 0.75)];
    [thumbnailFile saveInBackgroundWithBlock:^(BOOL success, NSError *error){
        if (!error) {
            weakSelf.product.thumbnail = thumbnailFile;
        } else {
            NSLog(@"error:%@",[error localizedDescription]);
        }
    }];

    [self.navigationController dismissViewControllerAnimated:YES completion:^{

    }];
}
```

In the implementation, a UIImage category method -(UIImage *)imageWithImage: scaledToWidth has been used.

```
+(UIImage*)imageWithImage: (UIImage*) sourceImage scaledToWidth: (float) i_width
{
    float oldWidth = sourceImage.size.width;
    float scaleFactor = i_width / oldWidth;

    float newHeight = sourceImage.size.height * scaleFactor;
    float newWidth = oldWidth * scaleFactor;

    UIGraphicsBeginImageContext(CGSizeMake(newWidth, newHeight));
    [sourceImage drawInRect:CGRectMake(0, 0, newWidth, newHeight)];
    UIImage *newImage = UIGraphicsGetImageFromCurrentImageContext();
    UIGraphicsEndImageContext();
    return newImage;
}
```

Enter Product Name, Price, Unit Price, and Product Summary

In general, it's an easy task to implement a UITextField or UITextView to accept a user's input. In reality, you need to consider that a software keyboard will occupy part of the screen. To handle this, I will introduce an approach that you will use a UIScrollView as a container view to hold all other UI controls. The purpose of UIScrollview is to help us move the whole view up while a soft keyboard is being shown. To do so, the first step is to add the method -(void)moveTextViewForKeyboard:(NSNotification *)aNotification up:(BOOL) up to the delegate methods of UITextView. When a UITextView begins the editing mode, you move the UITextView up for a software keyboard. When a UITextView finishes the editing, you move the UITextView down.

```
- (void)textViewDidBeginEditing:(UITextView *)textView {
    [self moveTextViewForKeyboard:nil up:YES];
}

- (BOOL)textViewShouldEndEditing:(UITextView *)textView
{
    [self moveTextViewForKeyboard:nil up:NO];
    return YES;
}
```

Next, implement how you can move a UITextView up and down. You already known the height of a software keyboard in portrait mode, which is 216 points. The whole idea of moving the UITextView up or down is by changing its origin by amount of 0.7*keyboard_ height so you can leave room for the software keyboard. In the following implementation, I have also considered the case that a device is in landscape mode.

```
#pragma mark - Keyboard Event Notifications

- (void)moveTextViewForKeyboard:(NSNotification*)aNotification up:(BOOL)up {
    CGRect keyboardEndFrame = CGRectMake(0.0, 0.0, self.view.frame.size.width,
    KEYBOARD_HEIGHT);

    [UIView animateWithDuration:1.0 animations:nil completion:^(BOOL finished) {
        CGRect newFrame = self.view.frame;

        if (keyboardEndFrame.size.height >keyboardEndFrame.size.width)
        {   //we must be in landscape
            if (keyboardEndFrame.origin.x==0)
            {   //upside down so need to flip origin
                newFrame.origin = CGPointMake(keyboardEndFrame.size.width, 0);
            }

            newFrame.size.width -= keyboardEndFrame.size.width * (up?1:-1);

        } else
        {   //in portrait
            if (keyboardEndFrame.origin.y==0)
            {
                //upside down so need to flip origin
                newFrame.origin = CGPointMake(0, keyboardEndFrame.size.height);
            }
            CGPoint origin = CGPointMake(0, keyboardEndFrame.size.height* 0.7*(up?-1:0));
            newFrame.origin = origin;
        }
        self.view.frame = newFrame;
    }];
}
```

Last, you can also call a simple UIScrollView method to dismiss the software keyboard triggered by any UITextField or UITextView, while an admin drags the UIScrollView instance.

```
self.scrollView.keyboardDismissMode = UIScrollViewKeyboardDismissModeOnDrag;
```

Select Brand

A better user experience is one in which you let your admin select a brand from a list; this is how you can do that. You query the brands from the Parse back end in viewDidLoad. In my implementation, I use a method for this purpose:

```
-(void)fireUpBrands.
- (void)viewDidLoad {
    [super viewDidLoad];

    [self fireUpBrands];
    // Do any additional setup after loading the view.
    self.title = NSLocalizedString(@"New Product", @"New Product");
```

```
    self.scrollView.keyboardDismissMode = UIScrollViewKeyboardDismissModeOnDrag;
    self.product = [EMABProduct object];

}
```

You also have to define NSArray properties, brands, and then a way to hold the query results. This is the implementation:

```
-(void)fireUpBrands
{

    __weak typeof(self) weakSelf = self;
    PFQuery *brandQuery = [EMABCategory basicQuery];
    [brandQuery findObjectsInBackgroundWithBlock:^(NSArray *objects, NSError *error) {
        if (!error) {
            weakSelf.brands = objects;
            weakSelf.brandTextField.inputView = weakSelf.brandPickerView;
        }
    }];
}
```

You query Parse to get all brands and let the inputview of the brand UITextField's inputView the instance of a UIPickerView.

```
-(UIPickerView *)brandPickerView{
    if (_brandPickerView ==nil) {
        _brandPickerView = [[UIPickerView alloc] initWithFrame:CGRectZero];
        _brandPickerView.showsSelectionIndicator = YES;      // note this is default to NO

        _brandPickerView.tag = 121;
        // this view controller is the data source and delegate
        _brandPickerView.delegate = self;
        _brandPickerView.dataSource = self;

        CGRect screenRect = [[UIScreen mainScreen] applicationFrame];
        CGSize pickerSize = [_brandPickerView sizeThatFits:CGSizeZero];
        CGRect startRect = CGRectMake(0.0,
                                    screenRect.origin.y + screenRect.size.height,
                                    pickerSize.width, pickerSize.height);
        _brandPickerView.frame = startRect;

        // compute the end frame
        CGRect pickerRect = CGRectMake(0.0,
                                    screenRect.origin.y + screenRect.size.height -
                                    pickerSize.height,
                                    pickerSize.width,
                                    pickerSize.height);

        // add some animation if you like
        _brandPickerView.frame = pickerRect;
    }

    return _brandPickerView;
}
```

You have the brands array; now let it be the data source of UIPickerView.

```
#pragma mark - UIPickerViewDataSource
- (NSInteger)numberOfComponentsInPickerView:(UIPickerView *)pickerView {
    return 1;
}

- (NSInteger)pickerView:(UIPickerView *)pickerView numberOfRowsInComponent:(NSInteger)
component {
return  [self.brands count];
}

#pragma mark - UIPickerViewDelegate

-(NSString *)pickerView:(UIPickerView *)pickerView titleForRow:(NSInteger)row
forComponent:(NSInteger)component
{
    if (self.brands && s[elf.brands count] > 0) {
        EMABCategory *brand= self.brands[row];
        return brand.title;
    }
    return NSLocalizedString(@"No Data", @"No Data");
}

- (void)pickerView:(UIPickerView *)pickerView didSelectRow:(NSInteger)row
inComponent:(NSInteger)component {

        EMABCategory *brand= self.brands[row];
        self.product.brand = brand;
        self.brandTextField.text = brand.title;

}
```

The UIPickerView's data source is the brand. When an admin selects a row, you let the row object be the brand of this product; you also show the brand title in the brand UITextField.

Save

In the view controller, you have set two bar button items on UINavigationBar. One is for "Save"; the other is for "Cancel." When an admin is ready to save the product information, the "Save" button can be tapped. Under the hood, you call the asynchronous method PFObject -(void) saveInBackgroundWithBlock:^(BOOL succeeded, NSError *error) to save the product to the Parse back end, and then leave the page. If any error occurs, you show the error.

```
-(IBAction)onDone:(id)sender
{
    [self.desciptionTextView resignFirstResponder];
    self.product.name = self.nameTextField.text;
    self.product.unitPrice  = [self.priceTextField.text doubleValue];
    self.product.priceUnit = self.unitTextField.text;
    self.product.detail = self.desciptionTextView.text;
```

```
        [self.product saveInBackgroundWithBlock:^(BOOL succeeded, NSError *error) {
            if (succeeded) {
                [self.navigationController popViewControllerAnimated:YES];
                [SVProgressHUD showSuccessWithStatus:NSLocalizedString
                (@"Saved  Successfully",@"")];

            } else{
                [SVProgressHUD showErrorWithStatus:[error localizedDescription]];
            }
        }];
    }
}
```

In the meantime, you dismiss this screen while an admin taps the "Cancel" bar button item.

```
-(IBAction)onCancel:(id)sender{
    [self.navigationController popViewControllerAnimated:YES];
}
```

Those are all the steps to implement this functionality. For the the sake of completeness, I have also added the header declaration, the delegate declaration in the class interface, and some other UI controls and properties.

```
#import "EMABAddProductViewController.h"
#import "EMABProduct.h"
#import "EMABUser.h"
#import <ParseUI/PFImageView.h>
#import "EMABAppDelegate.h"
#import "UIImage+Resize.h"
#import "EMABCategory.h"
#import "SVProgressHud.h"

#define KEYBOARD_HEIGHT 216.0

@interface EMABAddProductViewController ()<UITextFieldDelegate, UIGestureRecognizerDelegate,
UIImagePickerControllerDelegate, UINavigationControllerDelegate, UIPickerViewDelegate,
UIPickerViewDataSource, UIScrollViewDelegate, UIAlertViewDelegate>{
    UIImagePickerController * imagePickerController;
}
@property (nonatomic, weak) IBOutlet UIScrollView *scrollView;
@property (nonatomic, strong) EMABProduct *product;
@property (nonatomic, strong) EMABUser *owner;
@property (nonatomic, strong) NSArray *brands;
@property (nonatomic, strong) UIPickerView *brandPickerView;
@end
```

Summary

In this chapter, I talked about how to log in as an admin and how to add a product or edit one.

Chapter 17

Promotion

Push notification marketing is frequently used to promote discounts, deals, and new products. In general, creating the feature of push notification marketing can be quite complicated. A common use case is that once an app receives a push notification and a user taps it, the app will bring up the product page directly or a promotion section within this app. It will take quite an effort to establish features like this. However, we also have seen a use case like this: The user's device received a push notification; the user opens the app and then sees a promotion page. This page acts like a flyer and has content similar to "Check out our new products." Or "10% off for X'mas." Since the flyer page is an overlay on top of the main app, it can be dismissed with a tap. In this chapter, I will show you how to implement this behavior by using Parse's easy-to-use push notification feature.

Keep in mind though, to see this in action, you need to configure your app to receive push notifications with Apple Developer Portal and Parse, as introduced in Chapter 4.

Model

Create a new PFObject subclass for this promotion model and name it "EMABPromotion." It has two properties: one is for the promotion content, and the other is for the promotion image. Here is the header file:

EMABPromotion.h

```
#import <Parse/Parse.h>
@interface EMABPromotion : PFObject<PFSubclassing>
@property (nonatomic, copy) NSString *content;
@property (nonatomic, strong)PFFile *image;
@end
```

Next, register a new NSString constant kPromotion with the EMABConstants class. Also register the new EMABPromotion model with the AppDelegate class. Here is the EMABPromotion implementation file:

EMABPromotion.m

```
#import "EMABPromotion.h"
#import <Parse/PFObject+Subclass.h>
#import "EMABConstants.h"
@implementation EMABPromotion
@dynamic content, image;

+(NSString *)parseClassName
{
    return kPromotion;
}

@end
```

View

The promotion flyer view is pretty simple. Use a UILabel to show the content and a PFImageView to show the image, just like a flyer. Figure 17-1 shows what it looks like.

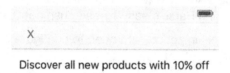

Discover all new products with 10% off

Figure 17-1. This is an example of a promotion flyer

Controller

Create a new UIViewController subclass, and name it "EMABPromotionViewController."
Here is the header file for this controller:

EMABPromotionViewController.h

```objc
#import <UIKit/UIKit.h>
@class EMABPromotion;
@interface EMABPromotionViewController : UIViewController
@property (nonatomic, strong) EMABPromotion *promotion;
@end

#import "EMABPromotionViewController.h"
#import "EMABPromotion.h"
#import <ParseUI/PFImageView.h>

@interface EMABPromotionViewController ()
@property (nonatomic, weak) IBOutlet UILabel *contentLabel;
@property (nonatomic, weak) IBOutlet PFImageView *imageView;
@end
```

Here is the implementation file, and it's pretty basic. Once you have an instance of
EMABPromotion, connect this model with the view. Let the content label show the
promotion's content, and let the image view show the promotion's image.

```objc
@implementation EMABPromotionViewController

-(void)setPromotion:(EMABPromotion *)promotion
{
    if (_promotion != promotion) {
        _promotion = promotion;

        [self configureView];
    }
}

- (void)viewDidLoad {
    [super viewDidLoad];
    // Do any additional setup after loading the view.
    [self configureView];
    self.navigationItem.leftBarButtonItem = [[UIBarButtonItem alloc] initWithBarButton
    SystemItem:UIBarButtonSystemItemDone target:self action:@selector(onDone:)];
}

-(void)configureView {
    self.contentLabel.text = self.promotion.content;
    if (self.promotion.image) {
        self.imageView.file = self.promotion.image;
        [self.imageView loadInBackground];
    }
}
```

```
-(void)onDone:(id)sender {
    [self dismissViewControllerAnimated:YES completion:nil];
}

@end
```

In the end, use a bar button item to dismiss the view controller when a user taps it.

Next, think about how to show the flyer view controller. The content of the flyer is sent with a push notification. The screen is shown when a user taps the notification. You need to move over to the EMABAppDelegate.

You know -(BOOL)application:(UIApplication *)application didFinishLaunchingWithO ptions:(NSDictionary *)launchOptions will be used in response to the user's tapping on a notification message, given that the app is in the background or has not added a helper method -(void)handlePromotion:(NSDictionary *)options.

```
- (BOOL)application:(UIApplication *)application didFinishLaunchingWithOptions:
(NSDictionary *)launchOptions {

    // Register EMABPromotion class
    [EMABPromotion registerSubclass];

    // Handle Promotion
    [self handlePromotion:launchOptions[UIApplicationLaunchOptionsRemoteNotificationKey]];

    return YES;
}

-(void)handlePromotion:(NSDictionary *)notificationPayload {
    // Create a pointer to the Photo object
    NSString *objectId = [notificationPayload objectForKey:@"p"];
    EMABPromotion *promotion = (EMABPromotion *)[PFObject objectWithoutDataWithClassName:
    kPromotion
                                                          objectId:objectId];
    [promotion fetchIfNeededInBackgroundWithBlock:^(PFObject *object, NSError *error) {
        // Show promotion view controller
        if (!error) {
            UIStoryboard *mainStoryboard = [UIStoryboard storyboardWithName:@"Main"
            bundle:nil];
            EMABPromotionViewController *viewController = [mainStoryboard
            instantiateViewControllerWithIdentifier:@"EMABPromotionViewController"];
            [self.window.rootViewController presentViewController:viewController
            animated:YES completion:nil];
        }
    }];
}
```

In this helper method, check for a promotion notification message. If yes, construct an EMABPromotion instance promotion based on one of the keys in the message content, the objectId. You need to do a little bit of remote fetching to get the entire content. Once the fetching is done, bring up the EMABPromotionViewController.

With Parse, it's just that easy.

Summary

In this chapter, I have introduced you to using push notifications to do a little bit of marketing. Basically, you implement a flyer page while a user taps a promotion push notification, then your app will query and load the promotion content from the Parse back-end server.

Chapter 18

Security

So far, I have discussed all of the features for an e-commerce iPhone app that I want to talk about except one: how secure the implementation is, or how safe it is to use Parse. I will use this chapter to cover the Parse security features and how you could follow some industry-standard best practices to make this iPhone app more secure.

Keys

As you have noticed, there are a few keys generated in the project dashboard after a Parse project is created. You have used the client key for this iPhone app and the master key in the Parse Cloud code. Keep in mind, the client key is not meant to be a security mechanism. This key is shipped with your app. Anyone will know what it is by decompiling your app and reading the source code or proxying network out traffic and seeing it on this app on another device. The same rule applies for those other keys such as the REST key, .net key, and JavaScript key, which are in the Parse dashboard.

On the other hand, you might have noticed that you need to protect the master key, as mentioned in Chapter 14. Just like its name sounds, a master key is like an admin password to your app's server. Keep in mind, don't include this key into your source code or check-in source control. Don't share it with others. In the Parse Cloud code, you only need to call the following method to use the master key:

```
Parse.Cloud.useMasterKey();
```

If your master key is compromised, you can reset it. Simply scroll down the page where you can see all of your keys, and then you will see how to reset your master key (see Figure 18-1).

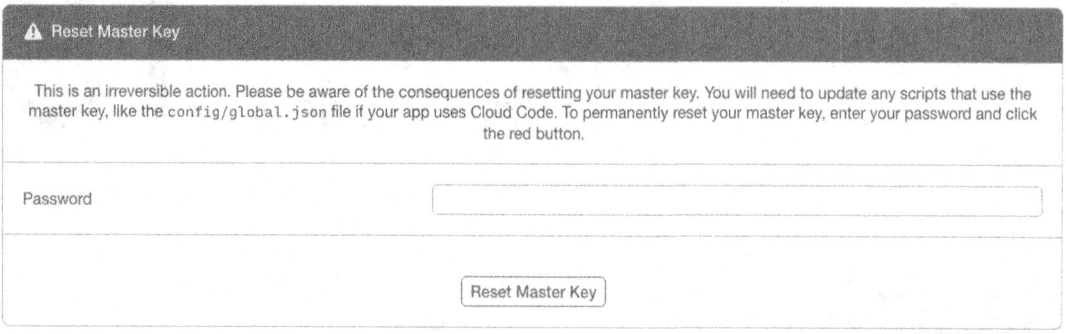

Figure 18-1. *You can reset master key*

Permissions

In this e-commerce app, most of your users can only read brands and products information. Only a few can create, edit, or delete a brand and a product. This is a typical use case of permissions.

Parse makes it easier for you to create class-level permissions. Almost every class that you create should have some read-write permissions to some degree.

To start with your class-level permissions, click on "Security" in the Data Browser for the class you want to configure (see Figure 18-2).

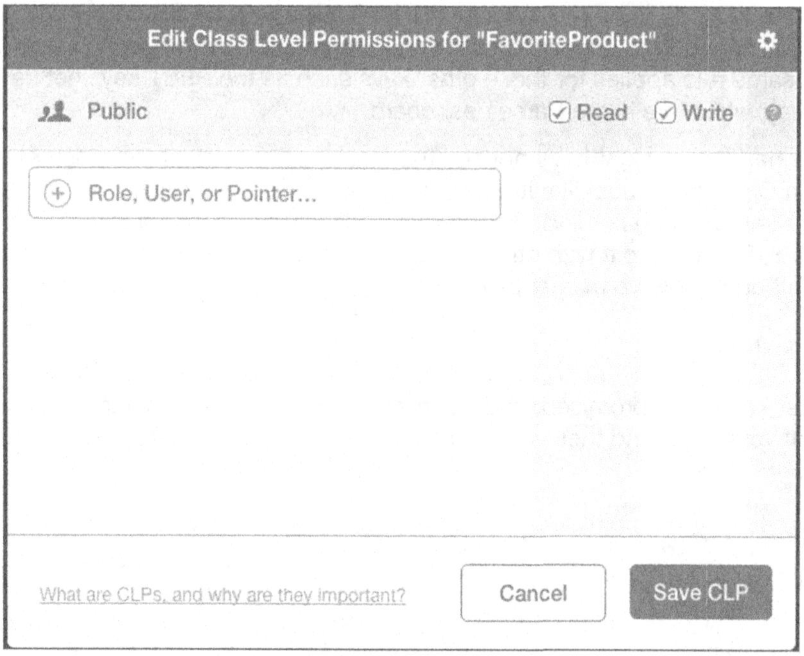

Figure 18-2. *Set the class-level permission (CLP)*

In the "FavoriteProduct" class, the default permission is that everyone can read and write this class, which fits your use case. However, the correct permission for the "Product" class should be "Read" for everyone, and "Write" for "a few." "A few" can be certain predefined Roles or Users. A Role is simply a set of Users and Roles who should share some of the same permissions. For example, you can set up a Role called "admins" and make a table writable only by that role.

While in development mode, the "client class creation" is automatically on, which is a great benefit for a developer who doesn't needs to leave Xcode to create a class with its properties. It's recommended to turn this feature off while your app is in production mode. Figure 18-3 shows how you can disable it.

Figure 18-3. App-level client class creation

Access Control List (ACL)

If an object doesn't have an ACL, it's readable and writable by everyone. The only exception is the _User class. You never allow users to write each other's data, but they can read it by default. To make it super easy to create user-private ACLs for every object, you have a way to set a default ACL that will be used for every new object you create.

```
[PFACL setDefaultACL:[PFACL ACL] withAccessForCurrentUser:YES];
```

And you put this line code in the method of - (BOOL)application:(UIApplication *) application didFinishLaunchingWithOptions:(NSDictionary *)launchOptions in AppDelegate.m.

Let me also go over some other common use cases you might need to handle.

The first and quite common use case is that you can set different read and write permissions on an object. For example, this is how you would create an ACL for a product review posted by a user, where anyone can read it:

```
PFACL *acl = [PFACL ACL];
[acl setPublicReadAccess:true];
[acl setWriteAccess:true forUser:[PFUser currentUser]];
[review setACL: acl];
```

The second case is a user's data, such as e-mail addresses or phone numbers. You don't want to let other users see each other's e-mail. To set an ACL on the current user's data that should not be publicly readable, all you have to do is this:

```
PFUser *user = [PFUser currentUser];
user.ACL = [PFACL ACLWithUser:user];
```

The third case is that you want some data created by a user that is public and some that is private; it's best to have two separate objects. You can add a pointer to the private data from the public one.

```
PFObject *privateData = [PFObject objectWithClassName:@"PrivateUserData"];
privateData.ACL = [PFACL ACLWithUser:[PFUser currentUser]];
[privateData setObject:@"555-5309" forKey:@"phoneNumber"];
 [PFUser setObject:privateData forKey:@"privateData"];
```

The fourth use case is that you only limit some super users to write other users' data, or if you don't want to manage permission per-user basis, you can use a Role object. Roles are a special kind of object that let us create a group of users that can all be assigned to the ACL. For example, you have an "admins" role, and you can let some users have this role. While you create a Review object, you let "admins" have the full permission of read and write. You can do the following:

```
PFACL *acl = [PFACL ACL];
[acl setPublicReadAccess:true];
[acl setWriteAccess:true forRoleWithName:@"admins"];
```

One of the benefits about roles is that you can add and remove users from a role without having to update every single object that is restricted to that role.

Last, if you, as the developer, need to update other _User objects, you can use Cloud Code combing with the user MasterKey option to do this.

Cloud Code

In this e-commerce iPhone app, I have shown that you can leave important functionality to the Cloud Code, which means you upload JavaScript code to your Parse project server. You call some functions to let Parse run it for you. This is different from the code for this iPhone app in that it is running on users' devices. This is much easier for people who want to modify your code. On the other hand, you can't always trust what a user has entered. The better practice is that you should validate the data that a user has entered; the right place is in Cloud Code so that you know a malicious client won't be able to bypass the validation logic you implemented for the client.

For instance, I have shown that you need to verify a user's e-mail address input before sign-up or login for this user in this iPhone app in Chapters 8 and 9. This practice makes for a better user experience purpose than does a security measure. In other words, you don't want to make an app call and then tell the user that the e-mail address entered is not valid. However, a hacker can easily bypass the client-side e-mail validation. The correct way to validate a user's input, Cloud Code has beforeSave triggers. These triggers can be used whenever an object is saved. You also have the chance to modify the object or completely reject a save.

For example, this is how you validate that a user has an e-mail address while signing up a user:

```
Parse.Cloud.beforeSave(Parse.User, function(request, response) {
  var user = request.object;
  if (!user.get("email")) {
    response.error("Every user must have an email address.");
  } else {
    response.success();
  }
});
```

On the other hand, there are other cases in which your users don't have full permission to write an object, but you want to bypass that limitation. For example, if you want to allow a user to "like" a "Post" object but the user doesn't have full write permissions on the "Post," you can implement this feature by using a Cloud Code function and useMasterKey option in your JavaScript code. With the useMasterKey option, you will override the limitation of writing or reading permission.

```
Parse.Cloud.define("like", function(request, response) {
  var post = new Parse.Object("Post");
  post.id = request.params.postId;
  post.increment("likes");
  post.save(null, { useMasterKey: true }).then(function() {
    response.success();
  }, function(error) {
    response.error(error);
  });
});
```

Last but not least, Parse has provided a great feature by allowing a client (for example, your iPhone app) to initiate sending a push notification. It provides some flexibility while developing your app. While your app is in production, it's best that you turn this feature off by disabling "client push" in your Parse project setting. The reason is the same: you can't trust the behavior from your app. Instead, you should validate the data that will be sent by your Cloud Code functions.

Sessions

While a user is logged into your app through multiple devices, the Parse Cloud will assign a unique revocable Session object on a given device for your app. This means different devices and your browsers will have different session tokens for the same user. On mobile and your apps, you don't have to worry about creating and destroying sessions. When users log in or sign up, the Parse Cloud automatically creates the corresponding Session object. When users log out, the Parse Cloud automatically destroys the corresponding Session object, which invalidates the session token that was previously assigned to that user's device.

Parse also introduces a flexible Revocable Sessions API that lets you easily understand and securely manipulate user sessions in your app. You can see your app's Session objects in Data Browser, just like any other Parse object. If a user contacts you about his or her account being compromised, you can use the Data Browser, REST API, or Cloud Code to forcefully revoke user sessions using the Master Key. In addition, for increased security, you can configure your apps to automatically expire user sessions due to inactivity.

> **Note**   Futher information, visit an excellent blog series from Parse at `http://blog.parse.com/learn/engineering/parse-security-i-are-you-the-key-master/`.

Summary

In this chapter, I talked about the security mechanism Parse provides to secure your apps and users' data. Namely, they are Class-Level Permission, Access Control List (ACL), Cloud Code, and Revocable Sessions. Keep in mind they are not independent from each other. Most likely, you'll need to use all those approaches in a real-world production-ready app.

> **Note**   To read more about Parse security, please visit `https://parse.com/docs/data`

Chapter **19**

More from Parse

In Chapter 8, I introduced the sign-up feature. But how do you know whether the user has entered a valid e-mail? You need to do some verification to make sure the e-mail address the user entered is a valid e-mail address format. But you don't really do anything to make sure the e-mail address actually belongs to the user. In the world of e-commerce, e-mail marketing proves to still be effective. So you need a way to verify the e-mail while a user is signing up.

Luckily, Parse also thought about those common use cases and provided easy solutions. Let's dive into the e-mail verification process.

E-Mail Verification

To begin, enable the e-mail verification feature under Settings > Email in your project Parse Dashboard, as shown in Figure 19-1.

Verify user emails ⑦   Yes ⬤ ✓

Figure 19-1. *Enable Verify user e-mail feature*

Next, in your EMABUser model, add a new Boolean property: `emailVerified`:

`@property (nonatomic, assign) BOOL emailVerified;`

Also add this property to the `@dynamic` declaration in the EMABUser.m file.

Next, create an e-mail verification request e-mail template, as shown in Figure 19-2.

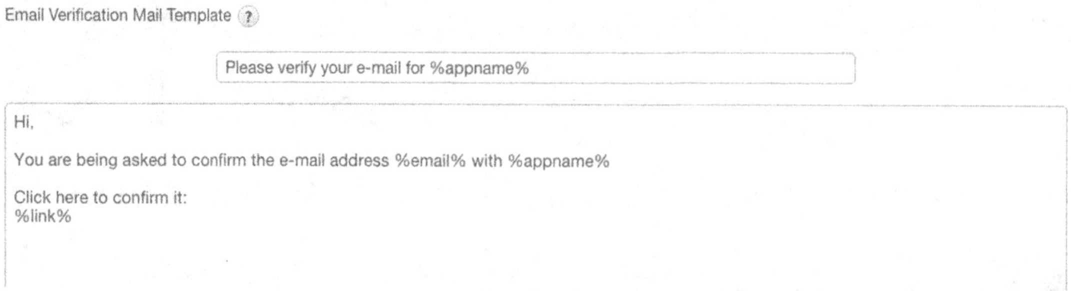

Email Verification Mail Template ⑦

Please verify your e-mail for %appname%

Hi,

You are being asked to confirm the e-mail address %email% with %appname%

Click here to confirm it:
%link%

Figure 19-2. This is an E-mail verification e-mail template

You can add or edit the content as you wish. Make sure you don't change the following URL, shown in Figure 19-3, if you don't want to host the template on your own server.

Custom 'email verified' page (template) ⑦

/apps/verify_email_success.html

Figure 19-3. This is an example e-mail verified page URL

Now, when you want to check whether the user has verified his or her e-mail, use the property in this way:

```
if (self.user.emailVerified) {
                // we proceed ahead
            } else {
// we ask this user 's verify it
UIAlertView *emailAlert = [[UIAlertView alloc] initWithTitle:NSLocalizedString(@"Email
Verification Request",@"") message:NSLocalizedString(@"Your email has not been verified,
please verify it to finish signing up.",@"") delegate:nil cancelButtonTitle:NSLocalized
String(@"OK ",@"") otherButtonTitles:nil, nil];

                [emailAlert show];

}
```

You still need a user to verify the e-mail. This user might have deleted the verification e-mail accidently, but now he or she is asking us to resend it. How do you this?

Basically, the solution is to set the "e-mail" property of the user as the same e-mail address you have on file, then save the user. Once saved successfully, it will trigger a resending of a verification e-mail to the e-mail address the user has provided. Here is the code:

```
if (!self.user.emailVerified) {
    UIAlertView *emailAlert = [[UIAlertView alloc] initWithTitle:NSLocalized
    String(@"Email Verification Request",@"") message:NSLocalizedString(@"Your
    email has not been verified, please verify it to finish signing up.",@"")
    delegate:self cancelButtonTitle:NSLocalizedString(@"Resent it",@"") otherButtonTitles:
    NSLocalizedString(@"OK",@""), nil];
```

```
                emailAlert.tag = 99;
                [emailAlert show];
        }

-(void)alertView:(UIAlertView *)alertView clickedButtonAtIndex:(NSInteger)buttonIndex
{
    if (buttonIndex == alertView.cancelButtonIndex) {
        [alertView dismissWithClickedButtonIndex:buttonIndex animated:YES];
    } else if (alertView.tag == 99){
        if (buttonIndex == 1) {
            [alertView dismissWithClickedButtonIndex:buttonIndex animated:NO];
        } else if (buttonIndex == 0){
            NSString *email = self.user.email;
            [self.user setEmail:email];
            [self.user saveEventually:^(BOOL succeeded, NSError *error) {
                if (!error) {
                    [SVProgressHUD showSuccessWithStatus:[NSString stringWithFormat:@"%@
                    %@.", NSLocalizedString(@"An verification email has been sent
                    to",@""),self.useremail]];
                }
            }];
        }
    }
}
```

Password Reset

On the other hand, you have implemented the feature to allow a user login in Chapter 9. What if the user forgets his or her password? As you have noticed from the Parse Dashboard, developers can't see a user's password either. You won't be able to tell the user his or her password. So you need a way to help the user recover or reset his password when needed.

The flow for password reset is as follows:

1. User requests that typing in his or her e-mail resets the password.

2. Parse sends an e-mail to the address, with a special password reset link.

3. User clicks on the reset link and is directed to a special Parse page that will allow him or her to type in a new password.

4. User types in a new password. The password has now been reset to the value specified.

On the login screen, add a new button with the title "Forgot password?" Once a user taps this button, execute a password reset action; bring up an alertView and let the user enter his or her e-mail address; a password reset instruction will be send to this email address. Here is the implementation for asking for the user's e-mail address:

```
- (IBAction)onPasswordReset:(id)sender
{

    UIAlertView *alertView = [[UIAlertView alloc] initWithTitle:NSLocalizedString
    (@"Password Reset",@"") message:NSLocalizedString(@"Enter your email to reset
    password",@"") delegate:self cancelButtonTitle:NSLocalizedString(@"Cancel",@"")
    otherButtonTitles:NSLocalizedString(@"Reset",@""), nil];
    alertView.alertViewStyle = UIAlertViewStylePlainTextInput;
    UITextField *emailField = (UITextField*)[alertView textFieldAtIndex:0];
    emailField.placeholder = NSLocalizedString(@"Email",@"");
    [alertView show];
}
```

Next, implement the alertView delegate method:

```
-(void)alertView:(UIAlertView *)alertView clickedButtonAtIndex:(NSInteger)buttonIndex
{
    if (buttonIndex == alertView.cancelButtonIndex) {
        [alertView dismissWithClickedButtonIndex:buttonIndex animated:YES];
    } else {
        UITextField *emailField = (UITextField*)[alertView textFieldAtIndex:0];
        [PFUser requestPasswordResetForEmailInBackground:emailField.text block:^(BOOL
        succeeded, NSError *error) {
            if (!error) {
                [SVProgressHUD showSuccessWithStatus:NSLocalizedString(@"Password reset
                instruction sent", @"Password reset instruction sent")];
            }

        }];
    }

}
```

The code above calls the PFUser's +(void) requestPasswordResetForEmailInBackground method. Parse will take care of sending a password reset instruction e-mail to this user's e-mail address.

Likewise, Parse has created an e-mail template for us, as shown in Figure 19-4.

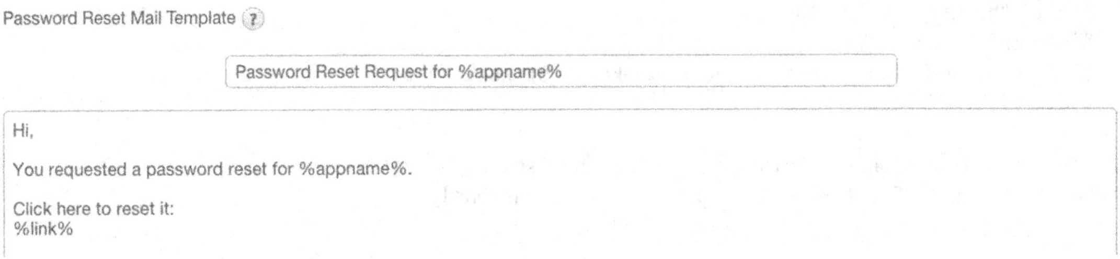

Password Reset Mail Template ⑦

Password Reset Request for %appname%

Hi,

You requested a password reset for %appname%.

Click here to reset it:
%link%

Figure 19-4. This is an example password reset e-mail template

Also notice that Parse has provided the "choose password" and "password reset success" URLs, as shown in Figure 19-5.

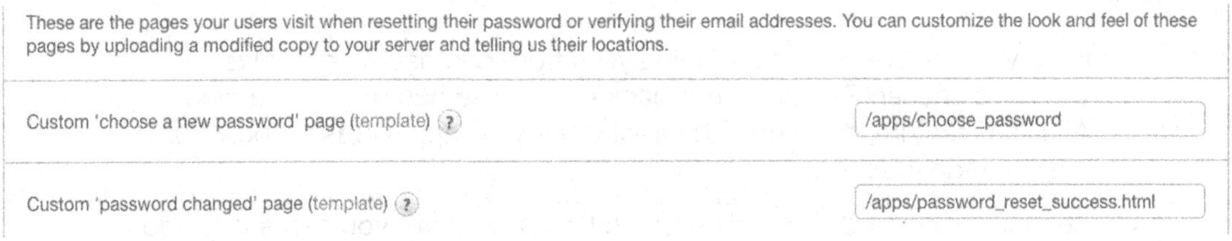

These are the pages your users visit when resetting their password or verifying their email addresses. You can customize the look and feel of these pages by uploading a modified copy to your server and telling us their locations.

Custom 'choose a new password' page (template) ⑦

/apps/choose_password

Custom 'password changed' page (template) ⑦

/apps/password_reset_success.html

Figure 19-5. Here are sample URLs for "choose a new password" and "password changed" page

If you want to upload these templates to your own server, hide parse.com from users.

Analytics

Parse provides a number of hooks for you to get a glimpse into the ticking heart of your apps. Without having to implement any client-side logic, you can view real-time graphs and breakdowns (by device type, Parse class name, or REST verb) of our API requests in your app's dashboard and save these graph filters to quickly access just the data you're interested in.

Parse App-Open & Push Analytics hook allows you to track the application being launched. By adding the following line to `applicationDidFinishLaunching:`, you'll begin to collect data on when and how often your application is opened.

```
[PFAnalytics trackAppOpenedWithLaunchOptions:launchOptions];
```

Graphs and breakdowns of your statistics are accessible from your app's dashboard.

PFAnalytics also allows you to track free-form events, with a handful of NSString keys and values. These extra dimensions allow segmentation of your custom events via your app's dashboard. Say your apps offer search functionality for apartment listings, and you want to track how often the feature is used, with some additional metadata. Here is the code:

```
NSDictionary *dimensions = @{
  // Define ranges to bucket data points into meaningful segments
  @"priceRange": @"1000-1500",
```

```
  // Did the user filter the query?
  @"source": @"craigslist",
  // Do searches happen more often on weekdays or weekends?
  @"dayType": @"weekday"
};
// Send the dimensions to Parse along with the 'search' event
[PFAnalytics trackEvent:@"search" dimensions:dimensions];
```

Crash Report

The Parse Crash Report iOS SDK is a great way for Parse developers to understand crashes after apps are downloaded and used by users. There are a few libraries that existed that can help track iOS app's crash and generate reports, namely, Crashlytics and Apple's Xcode Crash Report feature. The nice things about Parse's crash report, in my opinion, are threefold:

■ First, you can see all data and analytics from one dashboard, given you have chosen Parse as your back end. Parse has provided a nice Analytics feature, and you can directly see your app's crash report from the same dashboard.

■ Second, compared to Xcode's Crash Report feature, you can easily add members to the Parse project so a member who doesn't have Xcode installed still can easily browse crashes and mark them as solved. It's a great feature if you have a dedicated QA team. On the other hand, Xcode is mandatory if you choose to use Xcode's Crash Report.

■ Third, Parse tracks crashes on a per-version basis. If you have introduced an old bug in new version of your app, Parse lets you notice that old bug easily so you can fix it quickly, even if you've marked it as "resolved."

To include the Parse Crash Report iOS SDK in your project, use CocoaPods by adding this line into our podfile:

```
  pod 'ParseCrashReporting'
```

Then run 'pod update'; you should have it included into your project.

Next, enable the ParseCrashReporting in your EMABAppDelegate before setting Parse Application ID and the client key.

```
// Enable Crash Reporting
[ParseCrashReporting enable];
// Setup Parse
[Parse setApplicationId:@"YOUR-PARSE-APP-ID" clientKey:@"YOUR-PARSE-APP-CLIENT-KEY"];
```

After that, configure your project to send Parse the symbol files for each build of your apps. This allows Parse to properly aggregate crash incidents together and show these crashes on the dashboard with proper symbols in the stack trace. To automatically upload symbol files for your application whenever you build your app, initialize a new Parse Cloud Code directory by running the following (for example, in the same directory as your Xcode project):

```
parse new
```

Add a new Run Script phase to the Build Phases of your App's target:

```
export PATH=/usr/local/bin:$PATH cd <path_to_cloudcode_folder>  parse symbols <app_name_
from_cloud_code_config_globals> --path="${DWARF_DSYM_FOLDER_PATH}/${DWARF_DSYM_FILE_NAME}"
```

That's all you need to do.

Summary

In this chapter, I have introduced e-mail verification upon a user's sign-up, and how you could reset a user's password by uploading some templates to your own server. I introduce the Parse Analytics briefly. At the end, I also introduced Parse's crash report feature so that you can see the crash history in Parse Dashboard.

Index

P, Q

U, V, W

X, Y, Z

Get the eBook for only $5!

Why limit yourself?

Now you can take the weightless companion with you wherever you go and access your content on your PC, phone, tablet, or reader.

Since you've purchased this print book, we're happy to offer you the eBook in all 3 formats for just $5.

Convenient and fully searchable, the PDF version enables you to easily find and copy code—or perform examples by quickly toggling between instructions and applications. The MOBI format is ideal for your Kindle, while the ePUB can be utilized on a variety of mobile devices.

To learn more, go to www.apress.com/companion or contact support@apress.com.

Printed in the United States
By Bookmasters